ENDORSEMENTS

Shame attempts to convince us that we are damaged, and therefore we should continue to hide. Carl Thomas knows these adverse effects of sexual shame not only as a national leader helping men heal from unwanted sexual behaviors, but also from his own twenty-year struggle with porn. *When Shame Gets Real* is for people seeking a remedy from the painful experience of sexual shame. Carl's book can help you move beyond a mere desire to outgrow a behavior and into the stories and dynamics that reinforce it. Let this book support your journey to freedom through guiding you to disarm the debilitating power of shame.

—**Jay Stringer, Psychotherapist and author of**
Unwanted: How Sexual Brokenness Reveals our Way
to Healing

This shouldn't be rocket science, but somehow the church has forgotten—you can't cure shame by feeding shame. And so Carl Thomas doesn't just pull back the curtain on shame around porn and masturbation; he yanks the curtain down, rips it to shreds, and burns it. And it's about time! This book will help men get real with what is holding them back from wholeness, and it leads to true emotional, spiritual, and relational health. Thank you for this gift to men, and women, who have lost hope.

—**Sheila Wray Gregoire, author of *The Great Sex Rescue*,**
and podcaster and blogger at Bare Marriage

Everyone needs a Carl Thomas in their life. Someone who talks about the stuff most of us won't. Not to be crass or irreverent, but to push us toward growth and transformation. That's his passion. It's also the goal of *When Shame Gets Real*. If shame has ever held you back or quietly whispered, "You're worthless," I have a suggestion: Shut its mouth by diving into this very raw and honest book. Your transformation—a bigger, bolder, more powerful life—is about to get real.

—Jeff Borkoski | Best Selling Author of *Wife Magnet: Become the husband she cant keep her hands off*

When Shame Gets Real is a breath of fresh air for those who are sick and tired of getting hollow answers to their questions about sexuality, especially in a faith context. Carl is inspiringly honest, ridiculously down to earth, and minces no words as he explains the destructive impact of shame from several angles while also demonstrating what it looks like to deshame by sharing his personal stories in great detail. His humor and straightforward writing will keep your guard down, give you permission to look within without being judged, and lead you further down the path of sexual integrity and farther away from the lonely caverns of shame.

—Sathiya Sam | Founder of DeepClean Coaching and Author of *The Last Relapse*

Shame is crippling to the mind and soul. Carl does a good job of describing what shame is and the many ways it damages individuals and relationships. His writing style is raw and real. If you have struggled to break free from unwanted sexual behaviors and maybe never understood why, this book can help you.

—**Jonathan Daugherty | Founder at Be Broken Ministries**

WHEN SHAME GETS REAL

A new way to talk about sex, porn, and masturbation

CARL THOMAS

FREILING
PUBLISHING

Copyright © 2022 by Carl Thomas
First Paperback Edition

All rights reserved. No part of this publication may be reproduced, distributed, or transmitted in any form or by any means, including photocopying, recording, or other electronic or mechanical methods, without the prior written permission of the publisher, except in the case of brief quotations embodied in critical reviews and certain other noncommercial uses permitted by copyright law. For permission requests, write to the publisher, addressed "Attention: Permissions Coordinator," at the address below.

Some names, businesses, places, events, locales, incidents, and identifying details inside this book have been changed to protect the privacy of individuals.

Published by Freiling Publishing,
a division of Freiling Agency, LLC.

P.O. Box 1264
Warrenton, VA 20188

www.FreilingPublishing.com

PB ISBN: 978-1-956267-28-0
e-Book ISBN: 978-1-956267-29-7

CONTENTS

Introduction   i

1   Meet the World's Biggest Liar   1

2   Your Own Worst Enemy   17

3   The Universal Tie that Binds   31

4   Sacred Sexuality   47

5   The Silence that Kills   69

6   Anti-Social Media Malaise   87

7   The Privacy Myth   101

8   Well, That Was Awkward—
      A Lesson in Values   119

9   That Cuts Deep   141

10   Gut Check Time   161

11   Deep Work   181

12   The Road Ahead   201

Additional Resources   223

Notes   229

INTRODUCTION

May 6, 2012
Sunday 7:00 AM

I remember that day so clearly. It started off like any other "normal" Sunday for me and my family...

> Get up.
> Eat breakfast.
> Drink coffee.
> Help my wife get the kids ready for church.
> Hustle off trying to make the beginning of services on time.

Nothing out of the ordinary at all.

Except one major thing: **That very day, an article came out in our largest local paper titled "Putting an X through XXX."**

Below the headline was a color photo of me wearing the "Jesus Loves Pornstars" t-shirt that I had sported at multiple outreach events with XXXchurch.com.

Then below the photo was this excerpt:

> "You can't miss me," Carl Thomas says, and he's right: No one else at the diner is wearing a "Jesus

> Loves Porn Stars" t-shirt from the XXXchurch. "I appreciate outside-the-box ministries," explains the Deptford resident, a born-again Christian who helps other men overcome what they experience as a soul-destroying dependence on pornography.

The article focused on the work I was doing in the area with a local porn addiction recovery group that I had launched without the help of my church, and my volunteer mission efforts with a prominent sex and porn-focused online ministry.

I know, I know—making the paper. Pretty cool, right?

Yeah, except this interview dove into all sorts of things beyond my volunteer work with XXXchurch **such as the fact that I had my own unfortunate battles with pornography.**

For anyone else (or even me ten years later), the article's reference to my previous struggles with porn seemed innocuous enough.

> He speaks from personal experience. "I can tell you that a life with porn and a marriage is so inferior to a life without porn and a marriage," Thomas says. "It's definitely something I've had in my life, without going into details."

But as a guy who had only recently found freedom from my 20+ year addiction, it felt like the focus of the entire piece. Those two sentences (from my perspective) might as well have been a huge neon billboard that flashed: ATTENTION:

CARL WAS A HOPELESS PORN-ADDICTED PERVERT, TOO!

Understand that leading up to that interview, I knew I'd be talking about my struggles with porn, but the reality of how that would feel when it got printed didn't hit me until that moment.

The fact that I was being afforded an amazing opportunity to share my story and bring attention to a serious issue was almost completely overshadowed, in my mind, by the knowledge that I had just revealed one of the most personal, and quite frankly embarrassing, aspects of my life to anyone who had eyes and could read.

There was no retraction.
There was no going back.
There was no undoing what was now public information.

There was only the reality that in a couple of hours, my wife and I were going to be attending our local church with a bunch of people who didn't know much about me, except for the fact that I had struggled with porn.

That's a great way to start off a conversation over coffee, right? I could picture the whole awkward scenario:

> Hello, my name is Carl. What's your name?

> I'm Bob. Nice to meet you. Hey, aren't you the guy in the paper who struggled with porn and masturbation?

> Yep, that's me. Wanna shake hands?
>
> Nah, I'll pass, but thanks.
>
> OK, pass the creamer, please.

I'm not going to lie. There was a heavy mix of excitement and anxiety that ran through me and my wife on that drive to church, because we knew that nothing after that day would be the same.

Everybody would know about my struggle from our pastors, to our small group of friends, to people who'd never said a word to us at our church, to our parents and extended family, to even the bagger at the local grocery store.

There was no running away from the reality that I had just exposed a part of my life that I had spent the majority of my years trying to hide.

The truth was that morning, shame got very real for me.

And it got real for my wife, too.

Yeah, my past porn use was about me and my choices. But for my wife, it was a reflection on our marriage and her as a partner:

> What would other women think?
>
> Clearly I was drawn to porn because she couldn't satisfy me.

Obviously there was something lacking on her part.

Or at least those were some of the thoughts she was struggling with.

We got to church that morning, and to the surprise of both of us, nothing was that far off from the norm.

No special parking spot for the masturbator and his wife.
No scarlet letter for us to wear and share.
No one trying their best to avoid eye (or hand) contact.

But then it happened…

"Hey Carl, I saw your article in the paper!"

"Oh, great," I replied, uncertain of what was about to come next.

"Man, great job. Love what you are doing!"

My wife and I looked at each other and smiled, both relieved. But then someone else came up and said something, and then someone else, and then someone else. And the crazy thing was that each and every conversation was amazing and encouraging.

Not a single negative comment.

Not one awkward stare.

Nothing remotely as bad as what I had imagined happening.

It was like all those negative, self-condemning thoughts I had whipped up in my head were just that—*in my head.*

The truth was we both had a choice to make that morning.

We could cave to the pressure of shame and embarrassment that we were both experiencing, or we could use that opportunity to present our testimony and clear the way to help others who possibly were struggling with the very same things.

We could have turned the car around and watched an online service.

We could have lain low and avoided our friends and family for a few weeks until things blew over.

We could have claimed that the columnist misquoted me, or at the very least we could have minimized the truth of the matter.

We could have done all those things.

But we didn't. And thank God for that.

Let me be honest: *Shame is a bitch.* It doesn't give you a lot of options.

Shame cares about one thing and one thing only: suppressing you and everything that matters in your life such as your work, hopes, dreams, and passions. It wants to chase you into a little dark corner where you can stay hidden from the rest of the world, remaining ineffective and impotent.

Reality check: We all have moments in our life when shame will present itself to us.

For some, it may be a daily struggle.

For those who struggle with sexual brokenness, it's often a minute-by-minute struggle.

And so we all face a constant tension. Do we let shame take us down into its deep dark abyss of hopelessness? Or do we stand up to it and move forward, denying the power it tries to exude over us?

It's honestly a simple choice but with profound implications.

That day, if I had chosen the path of shame, or if I had never done the interview in the first place, I can confidently say my life would look nothing like it does now. I probably wouldn't be leading a ministry that reaches over 350,000 men and women a year dealing with their own sexual struggles and pain. Nor would I be witness to the thousands of people discovering a new type of freedom in their lives through the work of our online communities and resources.

Quite frankly, if I had chosen the path of shame, my life would not have the same purpose and passion that it does today.

It's shocking and often tragic how much shame impacts our lives, altering our destinies, hopes, and dreams.

In this book, I'm going to share some stories of shame and victory, from my own life and from people I know. My hope is that as you read this book, you will recognize:

> First, if shame has a hold in your life, you are not unique or alone. You are facing a very common struggle.
>
> Second, you have a choice. You can let shame have its way with you and how you live your life, or you can deny its power and stand up to its oppressive will.
>
> Third and finally, **IF** you choose to pursue a life free of shame, free of guilt, and free of embarrassment, you will unlock doors you never thought possible—doors of freedom, healing, restoration, and greater purpose.

Don't let shame have the last word in your life.

I hope what I have written here is going to inspire you and help you choose a better path, a shame-free path. Because, make no mistake, even if you read this entire book, there's a very good chance that shame is going to present itself to you in the near future, and at that point you will have a very critical choice to make.

What will you choose?

Chapter 1

MEET THE WORLD'S BIGGEST LIAR

I run a nonprofit ministry called Live Free. We offer resources for men, women, and spouses who have been impacted by porn addiction and other unwanted sexual behaviors. Our ministry is probably best known for its Live Free Community mobile app and our website/brand XXXchurch.

I got into this line of work because of my past experiences with this stuff, and also because I have seen firsthand how insidious and debilitating shame can be in the life of a person who struggles with these things.

One of the reasons I created the Live Free Community app, an online support and recovery community for men struggling with unwanted sexual behaviors, is that I believe if men cannot get past the shame of their poor choices, they will never find true freedom.

The reasons I believe this are many.

Regardless, the truth is that even within safe communities like the ones we've created, men (and women) still wrestle with shame even amongst others who are on the same journey.

For instance, I remember when one (now) long-standing Live Free member signed up and introduced himself to our community. Let's just call him Mike.

His post reflected a deep-seated shame and clearly articulated the impact that had on his life.

He wrote:

> *Two things I need to share:*
>
> 1) *I want to be safe. I want to risk being known and I don't want to pretend anymore. It's exhausting.*
>
> 2) *I deal with SSA [same sex attraction]. I've spent a lot of years hating this struggle **and hating myself for having this struggle.** I never felt like it was safe to share about some childhood abuse I experienced, and I just assumed that **if anyone found out "the truth" about me**, they'd hate me.*
>
> *I believed that about the church and the world. **When you assume that you're worthy of hate**, you don't expect anything better and you start to believe your own bad press and you hate yourself too.*
>
> *Been there, done that, bought the t-shirt, now ready to burn the t-shirt.*
>
> *I need to ask a favor right off the bat: I need your help to feel safe, and that even if you can't understand my struggle—you will fight alongside me. I've never felt*

accepted by the tribe of men, so at some point I gave up trying. But I never stopped wanting to belong.

Porn became my "false tribe," where I was always enough, never rejected, always valued, always wanted. But it wasn't even a little bit real. I want and need better. So, what do you say? **Can I count on you to welcome me in**, *to be a safe place and to help dismantle the lies I've believed for decades?*

Truthfully, when I read Mike's post I thought to myself, *"Man, I don't know if this guy is going to make it. How long will it be until he punches out?"* After all, I had seen similar posts like this from other newbies in the past, and nine out of ten times, they would be gone as quickly as they showed up.

His comments were so thick and laden with shame; it was clear that his "battle" with porn was a secondary issue.

Think about it—he was introducing himself to a community of men all dealing with the same sort of stuff. Yet somewhere deep inside of him was the misbegotten fear and belief that something was so wrong with him that not even other guys dealing with their own addictions could tolerate him. For some reason, he thought he was not worthy of love and acceptance from anyone, including his own peers.

Mike needed to conquer the shame in his life first and foremost if he was going to see any success.

He needed to recognize his inherent self worth.

He needed to get past the self-hate.

He needed to stop swallowing the lies of shame if he was ever going to move forward in victory and freedom.

An Unwanted Friend

I'll be honest, one thing that I can't stand is a liar.

Maybe it's because in the northeast we are a more "direct" bunch and prefer a punch in the mouth instead of a knife in the back, but regardless, **a dishonest character is something that I can't abide.**

Steal from me? That sucks.
Talk about me? Whatever.
Insult me? Try harder.
Cheat me? I got my eye on you.

But lie to me when I call you out? Now we gotta problem.

And listen, I get the fact that we all lie or have lied. I know when I struggled with porn, I lied all the time about my misdeeds (usually to my poor wife). And I'm not claiming any moral superiority here whatsoever.

But in my mind there is a difference between lying and being a "liar."

One is an action.
The other is an actor.

The problem with liars is that you simply can't trust anything they say. And if you can't believe what comes out of their mouth, there's nowhere to go from there.

Who cares about an apology if it's insincere?
Who needs a promise if it's never going to be kept?
Who wants loyalty if it's as fleeting as the afternoon breeze?
Who wants to build trust when there is no foundation to build on?

But yet, many of us still choose to pursue a relationship with one of the biggest liars the world has ever seen. Meet the friend you never needed.

His name is Shame.

Shame has been around for a long time. Longer than any of us.

And shame has been making friends and spreading its lies since the beginning of time.

In the Beginning...

Chances are, whether you're a Christian or have no faith context whatsoever, you know about the story of Adam and Eve and the Garden of Eden.

It goes something like this...

God created an amazing world we now know as planet earth. Adam and Eve were the first two people he made, and so he gave them a beautiful garden full of potential and teeming with life.

All of this was theirs for the taking but with one little caveat: **don't eat the fruit of one specific tree.**

Of course, we all know what happened.

They were tricked into eating the forbidden fruit by a cunning and clever serpent, which resulted in complete disaster—something the church world often refers to as the fall of mankind.

It's a beautiful story and yet a tragic one.

A promise of limitless potential that results in the worst ending ever!

We closely associate this chapter of human history with something we call "sin" or original sin. It's the story of man's disobedience to God, which resulted in a world that was once full of life but is now a place where people hurt and kill each other for gain and power.

But when I look at that story, not only do I see the extreme cost of disobedience, but I also see the grand entrance of our old "friend" shame.

In the Bible we read that after they ate of the tree, *"their eyes were opened, and they suddenly felt shame at their nakedness. So they sewed fig leaves together to cover themselves."*

Why did they feel the need to clothe themselves?

What gave them the urgency to hide and get dressed?

After all, at that point in history, there were no Euro models walking around making Eve feel bad about her saggy butt. Or Adonis-like actors whose six-packs made Adam want to hide his dad bod.

And let's be real, at that point, I am pretty sure both Adam and Eve had physiques that we all would have killed for since Chick-fil-A had not been invented at that point in history.

Regardless, when they saw each other naked for the first time, completely bare—flaws and all—they didn't like what they saw. Maybe they didn't like what they saw in each other. *But more likely,* they didn't like what they saw about themselves.

And so they bought into their new friend's lies and felt immense shame and the need to cover up.

The ironic thing is when God confronted Adam and Eve, it seemed that his primary concern was with their newfound need to hide and not what they had just done. I say that because his first question was:

Why are you hiding?

Followed by his second question:

Who told you that you're naked?

Of course, he knew the answer to both those questions before he asked, but it's evident that his concern had nothing to do with their poor but eco-friendly fashion choices. He was concerned about the fact that something had shifted in their consciousness, causing them to want to go get dressed and cover up.

That, in that moment, the people God had created and deemed "good" no longer felt that way. They had stopped trusting his good story and had begun writing their own tragic one.

Gone was their innocence.

Gone was their belief that God knew what he was doing when he made them.

Gone was the untainted and fully transparent relationship they had with each other and their Creator because a new player had moved into the scene that would change the game forever.

Shame had just set up camp, and he wasn't going anywhere any time soon.

Simple Definitions

So before we keep going, let's answer the question: *What exactly is shame anyway?*

After all, many of us recognize the word, but often I see people more confused than you might ever believe about its definition. So let's set some boundaries as we explore this topic.

Shame is not guilt.

Guilt is something that we all feel or have felt at some point in our lives. Usually it arises from a situation where we have done or thought something that we think is wrong, or someone has made us believe it is wrong, and so we feel bad.

Guilt is generally not a good thing because it's a *feeling* that hurts our spirit but leads nowhere except to a self-induced pity party. In other words, we feel guilty, so we just mope around about it until it goes away (hopefully).

Regardless, guilt is about what you did.

Shame is not conviction.

Conviction is very similar to guilt in that it stems from a thought or an action. However, unlike guilt, conviction is a feeling that arises because of our own values and beliefs. In other words, what we've done violates our core principles, and so we feel the need to make things right.

Conviction, when allowed to serve its purpose, can lead to repentance and restoration. It is decidedly a good thing and redemptive by nature.

And like guilt, conviction is also about what you did.

Shame, however, is a completely different animal.

Shame is not about what you did, or what you said, or what you thought.

It's about who you are.

It takes the spotlight off your poor decisions and puts it on you. Shame lies to you and says, *"If people knew what you did, they would never understand, and they will reject you like the worthless piece of crap you are."*

Shame attacks your very nature and identity.

Terrizzi and Shook put it this way in their article "On the Origin of Shame: Does Shame Emerge From an Evolved Disease-Avoidance Architecture?":

> *The experience of shame encourages self-evaluative ruminations that are degrading and pervade all aspects of the self (i.e., both physical and psychological). As such, the self is perceived as innately flawed. Thus, shame is a negatively valenced self-conscious emotion that results in global self-condemnation (Tangney, 1991; Niedenthal et al., 1994).*[1]

In other words, shame erodes your trust and belief that what God made is actually "good."

It whispers in your ear, *"You'll never be enough, so why bother? Just do your best to pretend you are better than we both know you are and pray like crazy that no one ever discovers otherwise."*

And when your posturing and pretending fall short? Shame tells you to hide and avoid the messy fallout.

Shame never leads to repentance or restoration. There is no happy ending to this toxic friendship—just pain, isolation, and a lifetime of regret.

Parasitic Relationships

You know that person? Maybe it's the leaching uncle, or your "friend" who's always conspicuously missing when it's time to buy the "next round," or maybe that past boyfriend/girlfriend who constantly seemed to have an "urgent need" that you and only you could help them with (usually involving some sort of money exchange).

We all know those people, or we've had to deal with them at some point: *parasites*.

I know, such a strong word, but a fitting one.

Parasite comes from the Greek word "parasitos" translated *"a person who eats at the table of another."* Its earliest usage in the English language traces back to 1539 when referring to a "hanger-on" or person who lives on others.

It is also a term we use to refer to certain types of organisms (such as ticks or tapeworms) that feed off another organism (i.e., the host). In these types of relationships, the parasite grows and gains strength by exploiting its host for food, shelter, and/or transportation, generally at the expense of the host's own wellbeing.

No one likes a parasite.
No one wants to be around a parasite.
No one desires to be in a parasitic relationship.

Yet, when it comes to shame, *that's exactly the type of "friendship" we are dealing with.*

Shame is a parasite. Plain and simple.

Yes, shame is a very powerful feeling. At times, its influence is oppressive and overwhelming. But shame can thrive only if it has a host to feed off of. Like all parasites, without that host organism, it will eventually wither away and die.

Understand, shame gets its strength from feeding off the lies and insecurities we carry around with us. That fear, anxiety, sense of worthlessness, past rejection, and self-condemnation we've experienced all provide the perfect fuel for shame's existence and malignant growth.

And once it finds that proverbial chink in your emotional armor? It looks for daily opportunities to expose it, making it seem larger than life itself.

Lost that promotion to another coworker?

Shame sweeps in and says, *"See, your parents were right! You aren't good enough, and you never will be."*

Dumped by your girlfriend or boyfriend?

Shame seizes the moment whispering, *"You never deserved that relationship anyway. You aren't worthy of love, and you know it!"*

Just slipped up and looked at porn again for the umpteenth time?

Shame chides in barking at you, *"Well what did you expect? You are a hopeless, perverted failure anyway! It was inevitable, so stop fighting it."*

And here's the kicker, folks…

When we fall for the lies of this ill-begotten friend, we not only feed it, but we also feed the host it survives on, creating a never-ending vicious cycle.

Nonpartisan Opportunist

Shame is an equal opportunity offender, make no mistake. It doesn't care who you are, what you've done, or where you are going. Nor does it factor in your faith, political preferences, race, creed, or sexuality.

But the reality is that some are more apt to indulge its beguiling whispers than others. Not because of any inherent weakness or genetic makeup on their part, but because society and culture have paved the way for those destructive lies through its ignorance and indifference.

Take for instance my friend Daniel.

Daniel is a well-respected and very successful attorney. Talk to him for just a few minutes, and you will immediately detect his wit, intelligence, and wisdom. In fact, many people would look at Daniel and envy his station in life.

Married, smart, healthy, and well respected. *What's not for anyone to love?*

Except Daniel carries with him a lifelong struggle with same-sex attraction (SSA) and SSA porn. Realize as a Christian man coming from an evangelical background, having same-sex attraction issues is almost as "bad" as being a person who enjoys clubbing baby seals ... almost.

Daniel knows that the church's approach to SSA in general has been extremely problematic. He realizes that Cristendom in general has dropped the ball when it comes to the entire LGBTQ conversation.

He gets all that.

But regardless of one's views on sexuality, the bottom line is that <u>for Daniel</u>, being attracted to men and watching SSA porn are both unwanted sexual behaviors. And so, even though he has made huge strides in this area of his life, Daniel still battles extreme shame whenever these types of thoughts or urges flood his brain.

I remember one day I called Daniel after a long stretch of him doing really well both sexually and emotionally. We got on the phone, and instantly I knew something was not quite right. His whole demeanor and spirit were darkened by something heavy.

Had Daniel gone on porn binge?

Had he sought out a male prostitute?

What could have this man so beaten and downtrodden?

We talked for several minutes, and finally he told me that he had direct messaged a guy who also had SSA issues and that their conversation had crossed some lines. Nothing crazy or over the top at all—just a little outside the bounds of what he thought was appropriate.

That being said, after they had chatted for a few minutes they both decided that things were going nowhere positive and discontinued their messaging.

Sounds like a personal win—*right?*

Not for Daniel.

He told me, *"Carl, I am so down. Even though I know better, I just keep hearing the words 'f***ing fag' in my head and feel hopeless and disgusting. I sometimes wonder if I'll ever be 'normal.'"*

Realize that Daniel is not homophobic or "anti-gay." It's just for him, this attraction he wrestles with is a millstone that tends to drag him down to the deepest and darkest parts of his soul.

As he went on, I just grew more and more frustrated. I thought to myself, *"How could a guy who has so much going for him fall for this type of self-loathing and debasement?"*

Did he see what I saw in him?
Did he see what others saw in him?

Hitting my breaking point, I spoke up:

> *Daniel, what the hell, man? You know this stuff is crap. These are just lies that you are falling for. There's nothing wrong with you. You are human, and humans struggle—that's all. If I was there, I might punch you in the face and then hug you after, because what you are doing to yourself with this shame stuff is so damaging. You know better, bro!*

We kept talking and I kept affirming that the garbage he was hearing in his head was just that: *garbage*. After about fifteen minutes, he thanked me for my Jersey-style pep talk and we hung up.

But that day, shame had scored a point in Daniel's mind.

The only question was, would he play its game in the future, and if he did, would he be prepared with a good counterattack?

Chapter 2

YOUR OWN WORST ENEMY

When I got Anthony's very first direct message, I felt a jolt of excitement and anticipation. Usually when I receive direct messages from Live Free members, they are notes of encouragement, expressions of gratitude for creating a place of safety, and sometimes requests for advice and help.

Regardless, I love interacting with the community of men we serve, so messages like Anthony's serve as a kind of spiritual caffeine for me.

I opened up Anthony's message. It read:

> *Hey Carl, thank you for founding this network. I am really struggling with being in a group. I know I am messed up, but I hate talking about it. I feel as though I don't have anything I enjoy in life which is why I look at porn. I don't know how to change things.*

Anthony's words hit me with a mix of emotions. After all, it excited me that he had finally found a place to seek help, but it also saddened me that his outlook had become so bleak and hopeless.

Recognizing that this type of mindset takes time to change, I responded with some brief encouragement:

> *Man, glad to be here for you. Talking about* [this stuff] *is exactly what you need to be doing, bro. You are messed up. So am I. So is everyone.*

My response was simple, having one goal in mind: **to help communicate that he was not alone.**

This was not my last interaction with Anthony, as it turns out.

Over the course of the next twelve months or so, he would send me messages every so often, sharing his frustrations, self-doubt, and plans to quit his recovery efforts in the face of his "hopeless" condition.

Each time I responded with some encouragement and affirmation, hoping that he would stick with it and not just check out.

Each time I wondered if there was any real hope for Anthony due to the overwhelming shame he clearly struggled with so deeply and refused to let go of.

The truth is that Anthony isn't that different from many men I help.

The frustrations and challenges he faces on a daily basis are the same as most guys struggling with porn and sex addiction. His "failures" and "setbacks" are not especially heinous or troubling; they are relatively typical of most men, if I'm going to be honest.

But Anthony carries around a burden of shame that is heavier than most. The weight is so oppressive and overwhelming that in its presence, he feels completely impotent and helpless. As a result, he has come to the mistaken belief that he is simply too broken and flawed to fix, that he is somehow not deserving or worthy of the freedom and hope that others like him have discovered for themselves.

This is what shame does. It steals all hope and bankrupts you of any sense of self-worth or value.

Unwanted Collateral Baggage

The real danger of shame isn't the shame itself (although that's pretty bad). It's all the stuff that comes along with it—the baggage, if you will.

As Terrizzi and Shook observe,

> *Shame has ... been described as "maladaptive," because it encourages dysfunctional behaviors, particularly behavioral avoidance (Tangney, 1991; Niedenthal et al., 1994; Orth et al., 2006). For example, when individuals commit a moral transgression, those who are prone to shame are more likely to respond with anger and avoidance rather than empathy and apology, which could repair the damage that is caused by the transgression (Tangney, 1991).*[2]

Or in normal speaking terms, shame encourages more bad behavior and compounds one's mistakes rather than leading to their repair and resolution. I see this all the time with individuals who struggle with porn and sexual addiction.

The common scenario goes something like this:

> Joe looks at porn.
>
> Joe feels really, really bad about his poor choice.
>
> Joe thinks to himself, *"Man, I do suck."*
>
> Joe goes and looks at porn again to get his mind off how "bad" he is.

Again, this is one of the main differences between shame and conviction. One leads to repentance, and the other leads to self-pity, hiding, isolation, and denial.

Regardless, understand that every person's response to shame can vary from situation to situation and from day to day. But it never results in a happy ending.

On some days, shame just drives one to indulge even more in unwanted sexual behaviors, further deepening the shame the individual already experiences.

On other days, it may create a sense of intense anger or frustration that will then be unleashed on some unsuspecting family member or coworker, stressing or damaging those relationships.

And in extreme cases, it may even drive a person to perpetuate unspeakable violence against the perceived source of struggle in an attempt to deflect one's own feelings of shame and disgust.

Witness the Atlanta spa shootings that took place on March 16, 2021.

For those of you not familiar with the Atlanta tragedy, here's a short recap.

On March 16, 2021, 21-year-old Robert Aaron Long purchased a handgun from a local firearms store. Only hours later, he walked into the first of three Asian spas/massage parlors, beginning a shooting spree that claimed the lives of eight people, six of whom were Asian women.

When this young man was taken into custody later that day, he informed the police that his motivation for this unspeakable act was his sexual addiction that was "at odds" with his Christianity. Ironically, Long had been a customer at two of the massage parlors, and he said they were a source of sexual temptation for him (and others).

Long claimed that he initially entertained the idea of suicide as a way out of his sexual addiction, but then he opted to target the three spas he shot up as a way to "help" others dealing with the same addiction by eliminating "the temptation." Apparently, his humanitarian concerns did not carry over to the people he killed in this horrific tragedy.

When these unfortunate events played out, news about the case spread like wildfire. Even though he was never charged with committing a "hate crime," there were many who felt his actions were motivated by racism.

Here's the thing: I am not a psychologist, nor do I have insider knowledge regarding Long and his mental processes. And while it is certainly possible this young man had a bias or hatred for Asians, his actions tell me one thing.

This was not a "hate" motivated crime. It was a "shame" motivated crime.

What Robert Long said and did coincides with a severely deepened shame prone mindset.

Follow along...

1) He struggled with sexual addiction, a behavior pattern that evokes immense shame for those dealing with it.

2) He came from a religious background and mindset that often can send confusing messages regarding sex, sexuality, and the way to achieve "purity." When these topics are handled poorly, they can cast a great deal of shame on the behavior itself and those practicing it.

3) He felt hopeless and even thought about killing himself. Unfortunately, he wouldn't have been the first man (or woman) to "'off'" himself because of his perceived inability to conquer his sexual demons. Again, shame leads to self-pity and self-hate—not sincere repentance or restoration.

4) But then he projected his self-hatred and shame onto the people/businesses he saw as the reason for his problems and acted out against them. In other words, he scapegoated the situation (i.e., avoidance).

This type of tragedy saddens me because it serves as a horrific example of how we live in a culture that would rather "blame" than "own," often because we haven't addressed the shame in our own lives.

- It is much easier to target your temptation than take responsibility for it.

- It is much easier to point fingers than look in the mirror.

- It is much easier to find a scapegoat than admit you are the goat.

Again, this is an extreme and tragic example of what can happen when we demonize what we see as the enemy rather than just taking care of our own house. But when we are deeply afflicted with shame, the last thing we want to do is address our own issues and face the inevitable internal conflict that results.

DANGER! Proceed at Your Own Risk

While the emotional and social consequences of shame are bad enough, the toll it wreaks on our body and physical health can be just as bad. Or to put it another way, when we chronically indulge shameful thoughts, we do so at our own physical peril.

But how could that be? After all, shame is just "in our head," so then how could it impact our physical health?

The key to answering this question is recognizing that our emotional and physical states are interconnected. In other words, what we experience physically affects us emotionally, and what we experience emotionally affects us physically.

Understand that shame is a threat, plain and simple. So when we feel shame, our brain and body respond accordingly just as it would in the face of any other threat.

Luna Dolezal and Barry Lyons expressed it this way in their paper "Health-related shame: an affective determinant of health?":

> *Threats to self esteem or social status, directly correlate with increased anxiety and heightened biological stress responses. The biological response to stress includes the release into the bloodstream of the individual of various hormonal and chemical mediators including the steroid hormone cortisol and immunologically active substances called pro-inflammatory cytokines (PIC). This response is similar to the "fight-or-flight" mechanism, which is an adaptive response that tells our bodies to flee when we are faced with physical danger. However, **chronic** or maladaptive elevations of these agents, resulting in immunological or endocrine dysregulation, can be harmful to [one's] health.*[3]

And while our brains and bodies were created this way for survival reasons, we weren't designed to live in a perpetual state of fight or flight. In fact, doing so exerts an extreme strain on our biological systems.

Consequently, chronic shame can lead to long-term health problems such as "weight gain, heart disease, hardening of the arteries, and decreased immune function."[4]

Fantastic!!! Right?

Of course the "fun" doesn't stop there.

As I mentioned before, shame usually leads to developing undesirable avoidance strategies rather than seeking resolution and repair. These strategies can lead to engaging in other harmful behaviors such as alcoholism, addiction, and eating disorders, all of which serve to "numb" a person against the pain of shame and further harm one's overall health.[5]

Stuck, Stagnant, and Self-Defeated

Perhaps one of the most damaging aspects of shame is its ability to rob an individual of resolve and motivation.

Whenever I talk to guys struggling with porn and the like, a term I hear far too often is "stuck," as in, *"Hey, I've been trying to beat this thing for years, but I just feel stuck."*

Not frustrated.
Not angry.
Not even fed up.

Stuck.

"Stuck" because shame has convinced them that they are helpless to change their lot in life and any effort to do so is only bound for inevitable failure.

So what happens? They lose all hope and the drive to change things. *Hence, "stuck."*

I saw this type of outlook play itself out through my many interactions with Anthony, whom I mentioned earlier. Whenever he would send me a message expressing his intentions to quit his recovery or just expressing his general frustrations, often there was some sort of reference to his loss of will or lack of "ability."

Here are just a few examples:

> *I've kind of just accepted living in sin at this point. It bothers me but not enough to change or suffer. I'm glad you have some stronger people in here who are willing to do what it takes.*

> *I don't have confidence in my ability to set and reach goals in any area of my life. It's hard.*

> *I tried to make some goals and I failed. No matter how hard I try, consistency seems to elude me.*

> *I really want to achieve certain things in my life, but I feel as though I don't have anyone in my life who really holds me accountable for these things. I wish I could say I could hold myself accountable on my own, but I haven't been able to.*

Now here's the thing: When reading Anthony's comments in a vacuum, one might have a hard time feeling empathy for him. After all, when someone seems willing to give up on himself, it can be hard not to write off such sentiments as evidence of laziness and/or apathy.

However, when you take the time to understand the tremendous shame Anthony experiences on a daily basis and the lies he's undoubtedly told himself over the years, Anthony's lack of drive to achieve his goals and self-confidence to do so is not only understandable, *it's practically a foregone conclusion.*

As Verbecke and Gavino note from their 2003 study on the self-regulation of shame and its effects on performance:

> *Individuals high in shame, or propensity for shame, withdraw themselves from situations which require goal achievement. In the work environment, if failure seems probable, some individuals will not accept or not try to reach their goals.*[6]

This is why one of the most damaging aspects of shame at the end of the day is its uncanny ability to completely erode and obliterate any sense of self-confidence, self-assurance, and the will to change that reality.

Struggling with chronic shame is like being punched in the crotch over, and over, and over again.

But here's the kicker...

The one punching you is you. And despite the pain, tears, and broken dreams, you keep punching because you inwardly believe that you deserve the punishment you are exacting on yourself and have no faith that you could stop even if you wanted to.

It's no wonder that so many men I work with who struggle with unwanted sexual behavior are devoid of any belief that they can actually find freedom, because they are victims of their own manufactured irony.

Shame leads them to the unwanted sexual behaviors they internally despise. Those behaviors in turn increase the shame they already experience. As a result of that shame, they lack any hope that they can eventually leave those behaviors in the past, which ultimately leads to more shame and more unwanted behavior.

All the while, they hold the key to their own freedom and don't even realize it.

"Cart before the Horse" Thinking

When approaching the topics of sex, sexuality, porn, masturbation, and the shame that surrounds these areas of life, I often feel as if I am walking into a "which came first—the chicken or egg" scenario.

What I mean by this is that an inextricable connection exists between our hesitancy to tackle these conversations and/or pursuit of these unhealthy behaviors and the shame that is created as a result. But, at the same time, it is the very presence of shame in our lives that pushes us toward isolation, withdrawal, and avoidance strategies (i.e., addiction) in the first place.

So then, how does one ever move forward?

Recognize that over the years, I've ministered to many men dealing with sexual brokenness. And one of the primary benefits I've often touted when encouraging them to seek freedom and recovery is the lack of shame they can finally experience when not loaded down with the weight of their poor choices.

But, as I've grown older (and hopefully wiser), I realize that addressing unwanted sexual behavior and shame in this way is almost backwards thinking.

Yes, less porn, less masturbation, less escorts and strip clubs should lead to less shame. But we need to address the presence of shame first to unlock an individual's full potential to seek and pursue freedom.

After all, when one is heavily burdened with shame:

- He finds it harder to reach out for help because he fears the potential of rejection.

- He finds it difficult to persevere because he doubts that victory is even possible.

- He finds it uncomfortable to be accountable for his slip-ups along the way because he doesn't want to further damage his already tarnished image.

- He finds it practically impossible to pursue goals in his life because every goal seems hopelessly out of reach.

And when he does find a modicum of success but then faces adversity or a setback?

He finds it twice as hard to return to his recovery journey efforts because doing so only further reinforces the misbegotten belief that he never had a chance in the first place.

We need to stop putting the cart before the horse.

We need to stop pursuing freedom from our unwanted behaviors in an effort to rid ourselves of shame; instead, we must seek to mitigate the shame already present in our lives so we can fully and effectively pursue the freedom we desire.

Chapter 3

THE UNIVERSAL TIE THAT BINDS

Once I had found freedom from my own porn addiction, my marriage radically changed. The trust level was higher. Our intimacy increased. And to be honest, I just became far less selfish with how I approached my wife and her needs.

But one thing that did not change for some time, as it turned out, was the shame my wife carried around with her because of my porn use.

Truthfully speaking, the idea of her feeling shame over my poor choices seemed a little crazy to me.

After all…

> ***It was I*** *who had wasted untold hours in front of computers trolling the internet for porn (usually with my pants unzipped).*
>
> ***It was I*** *who had often settled for masturbating to a computer image rather than pursuing intimacy and healthy sex with my wife.*
>
> ***It was I*** *who had consistently lied about my distasteful behavior.*

> ***It was I*** *who had failed in my attempts to quit over and over and over again.*

How was any of that on her? Why in the world would she need to find freedom from her own shame when I was the one to blame for everything? What I didn't realize at the time was that my choices communicated to her a message of dissatisfaction.

Dissatisfaction with her.
Dissatisfaction with her body.
Dissatisfaction with our marriage.
Dissatisfaction with our sex life.

And so my perceived dissatisfaction triggered a deep sense of shame within her, fueled by the lies she had told herself growing up concerning her worth, beauty, and value.

The reality is the reason I chased porn had nothing to do with her at all.

Good wife, bad wife, great marriage, bad marriage, good sex, terrible sex … none of it mattered because my attachment to porn and the escape it promised had been something I had sought for over a decade, well before we ever met.

But she didn't know that.

And even if I had taken the time to explain everything to her, it all would have fallen on deaf ears as long as I had continued to indulge my addictive behaviors.

Understand that shame is often experienced through a two-way exchange, because "hurt" people inevitably hurt other people.

The shame I had once sought to numb through my porn use led to choices that consequently hurt my wife and tapped into her own shame reservoirs. Given enough time and lack of healing, chances are she would have eventually and unintentionally passed that shame along to someone else because that's what shame does—it spreads like wildfire.

The Monsters We Make

There's no getting around it: shame is a real beast. It's an everyday Goliath we must all face at one time or another in our lives.

But here's the crazy thing. **It's a beast we birth and feed.**

Don't get me wrong—the source(s) of our shame comes from experiences outside our control such as interactions with parents, teachers, extended family, clergy, friends, or professionals who have expressed some level of contempt for and/or disapproval of us.[7]

As the Harvard Business Review notes,

> *From a psychological developmental point of view, shame can be seen as a complex emotional response that humans acquire during early child rearing. ... It is a very basic emotion: Children seek to live up to their parent's expectations, and failing to do so, experience shame. ... This kind of shame is very*

> *difficult to overcome. The formative wounds of childhood—scars from being teased, bullied, or ostracized by parents, peers, and others—can become fixed in our identity.*[8]

But the emotional response and feelings we face as a result of these formative experiences are internally created. And unfortunately, this is a natural phenomenon.

Understand that emotions are both biological and unavoidable responses to external stimuli. So when you experience any sort of stressor or change in your environment, there will always be some sort of emotional response that accompanies that event. It's inevitable and completely natural.

But the emotion that's evoked is going to vary from person to person based on one's life experiences and circumstances.

For instance…

Two children get their school report cards. Both receive a "B" for a math grade.

Student A comes from a nurturing home where the focus is on effort, not results. His parents often encourage, affirm, and applaud him, and when the effort is lackluster, they take the time to ask him questions and understand the potential reasons he didn't feel compelled to try harder.

There's a lot of good back and forth in this home. When the child is challenged, it is done in a loving manner, never resorting to guilting or condemnation. This boy, however, does tend to struggle with math, so for him, a "B" is a real accomplishment. Understandably, when he gets his report card, he experiences joy, surprise, and possibly anticipation (looking forward to his parent's reactions).

Student B is a different story, though.

His parents are very rigid and demanding. Nothing ever seems good enough, and they always focus on the child's results, damning anything else. His older sister is a real genius and has a history of academic accomplishments, so the expectation is that her younger brother should deliver the same stellar results.

When he doesn't, the parents predictably express strong feelings of disappointment, shame, and even disgust, most likely because of their own unresolved shame issues.

This boy is accustomed to getting A's in math—after all, that's the expectation. So when he gets a B, his emotional reaction is very different from the first boy. Rather than experiencing joy or surprise, he senses overwhelming fear, sadness, disgust, and of course, shame.

Two different boys.
Same external stimuli.
Two dramatically different emotional responses.

The reality is what student B experienced was entirely predictable. In fact, you might say it was a scientific certainty that student B would feel overwhelming shame in light of his less than perfect grade and home environment.

As Dr. Candice Feiring notes in her article "Emotional development, shame, and adaptation to child maltreatment":

> *Parental behaviors that arouse fears of abandonment and use love withdrawal as a discipline strategy are believed to play a role in the development of a shameprone style in children (M. Lewis, 1992; Potter-Efron,1989). The use of verbal disapproval, hostility, contempt, and physical abuse convey the message that the child's core self is a disappointment and unlovable because she or he has failed to live up to expectations.*[9]

Again, the experience of emotion is natural, unavoidable, and by design. After all, if humans went around making decisions and judgment solely on facts and figures, void of any emotional consideration, we wouldn't be human—we'd be robots.

But the emotional response is internally created by the individual. Likewise, the way we process those emotions (feelings) is also of our own making. Ergo, when we struggle with an avalanche of shame, we have to look no further than in the mirror for the originator of that crushing landslide.

Shame is, again, a monster. But it's a monster we create in our own mental laboratories.

The Perfect Storm

Looking back, I can now identify the seeds of shame in my life and how those events contributed in many ways to my long-term porn usage.

Recognize that my childhood wasn't "horrific." I didn't come from a broken home, suffer sexual molestation, or have parents who ignored me. This is not the part where I unload on you all my deep, dark secrets of abandonment and abuse. But the tapestry of shame I carried with me for years was subtly woven into my being from an early age.

My dad grew up a sickly kid. He suffered from scarlet fever, and because of his illness, he spent much of his childhood in bed. He loved football, sports, and all the typical things boys enjoy, but due to his health, he couldn't participate in most of these activities. He won't say as much, but I believe those formative years had a huge impact on his self-esteem and self-worth.

As a result, my dad was the type of man who always pushed hard for what he wanted, tried to control any situation he found himself in, and was quick to highlight his accomplishments in an effort to prove to himself (and everyone else) that he wasn't that weak, sick kid anymore.

His chronic need for self-validation spilled over into almost every aspect of his life, including his parenting style. I often heard about how he did this, and he did that, any time we talked about life and its many challenges—not because he was trying to belittle me or hurt me, but because he needed to prove himself to me. Whenever we talked about grades, work, and even sexual integrity, a common response I heard was: *"Son, I wouldn't ask you to do anything I haven't done."*

My father, rather than saying he was mad or angry, usually opted to express his "disappointment" with me when I did crap on the proverbial bed. And when I did get something right, he would often point to his accomplishments that mirrored and even eclipsed my own.

On top of that, my father was not shy or coy about his feelings when it came to other people who were deemed "losers" or failures. His standards were rigid and unforgiving.

As a result, I grew up with this extreme need to validate myself and seek his affirmation. After all, I didn't want to be just another loser in his eyes. And when that affirmation didn't come?

You guessed it—I felt shame and disgust with myself.

To complicate matters, I was a really skinny and short kid who was a super late bloomer. So, all throughout school, I was that boy anyone could physically push around. Yes, I tried to compensate with my big mouth and cutting sarcasm, but in the end, I wasn't a jock. I wasn't part of the "cool" kids' group (side note: I went to Christian school, so "cool" is a highly debatable term). And I had very little luck with the ladies.

All that said, affirmation from my peers was in very short supply as well.

So when I discovered porn at a young age, it was a welcome escape. I didn't need to prove myself to anyone. I didn't need to worry about rejection or being embarrassed. I had everything I needed to avoid facing the reality of my own inadequacies.

After I graduated from high school, I enrolled at a local state university. Unlike the small Christian and bizarre cliquey environment I had just come from, at Rutgers I had the freedom to do what I wanted and to find the type of friends I wanted. Eventually I joined a fraternity and finally found acceptance among a group of guys who looked nothing like the high school peers I had happily left behind.

Drinking, sexual promiscuity, and all the other things my religious background frowned upon suddenly became normal. And since I always felt like a fish out of water in the church world, I found myself embracing this new normal.

When I graduated from college, I ended up going to work for my parents in their insurance agency. I'm not going to lie—insurance was awful. I hated the job, but I felt that I was helping my family, and the job security was pretty dang good to boot.

Unfortunately, all my new friends had also moved into their new careers that appeared far more sexy and profitable than mine. Consequently, it didn't take very long for me to delve even deeper into my porn addiction as a way to numb the feeling that, once again, I had come up lacking.

The Gift that Keeps Giving

After one year of successful recovery, two years of seminary, ten years of marriage, and seventeen years of a career I resented, the day finally came when I chose to walk away from the insurance business and my family's agency.

My decision to leave, mind you, wasn't an easy one. I had no job lined up, no guarantee of a better career waiting for me, and no arsenal of tradeable skill sets to bank on. All I had was a master's in theology and seventeen years' worth of useless knowledge related to an industry I was leaving behind. Can you say irrelevant life experience?

That's when a new opportunity came along with an online ministry I had followed.

Understand that I had volunteered with this organization for several years prior and even had done some part-time work for them, helping grow an online support group program. I guess because of the work I had done with them, they offered me a full-time position.

I jumped at the opportunity.

The next seven years were a bit of a roller coaster, if I'm being honest. Working for an online ministry that moved fast and expected you to keep up or get swept away in the chaos was a constant challenge. I was always getting thrown into new projects and being tasked with learning new skills that I had minimal to no prior experience with.

But the real challenge wasn't the company's trial-by-fire approach to employee "training" and development. It was the culture. My new boss, from my perspective, shared many of the same qualities as my old boss (my father).

They both rarely said sorry.
They both had a hard time with giving affirmation.

They both were highly skilled at offering not-so-constructive "criticism."

Except my new boss wasn't my dad. Yet his not-so-gentle corrections when I "messed up something" were just as painful and damaging to my sense of self-confidence and worth as they would have been if he had been my actual father. Clearly, I had some deep-seated daddy issues to work though, but at the time, it just felt as if I were still a loser to some degree.

It wasn't until I hit my emotional limits, got some balls, and decided to bet on myself that I quit and walked away to venture out on my own. It's funny how emotional pain works. Sometimes it can be our greatest enemy, but it also can be the very catalyst that propels us in a new direction. Regardless, that decision (and some quality counseling) changed everything.

In 2019, I ended up launching my own ministry called Live Free and then acquired the small groups program I once led. It took time, but I eventually was able to get to the roots of my pain and low self-esteem and do some real healing, which made me far happier and mentally healthier. In time, I even came to grips with some of the deep resentment I had harbored for years against my dad and former employer and learned to forgive those sins of the past.

All that said, I've learned a lot about shame and the power it had on me over the years. Through all the pain, all the emotional swings, and all the ups and downs, I've been able to come through with a renewed sense of self and worth. But make no mistake—the lies of inadequacy still whisper in my ear from time to time. And to be honest, I think they always will. Shame doesn't just go away; it only goes into remission.

Understand that by sharing these experiences, I'm not trying to paint my dad or my ex-boss as the "bad guy" or myself as the tragic hero. I don't believe they are inherently awful people, nor do I feel their social and relational tactics were ever meant to intentionally harm me. *In fact, both men have shown me extreme kindness and generosity at various times throughout my life.*

But I believe that they both, as many of us do, carry around their own burdens of shame and inadequacy due to the pain and betrayal they've experienced at the hands of others in their lives. And like so many others out there, they are just trying to manage that pain the best way they can.

Hurt people hurt people.

The gift keeps giving.

Enough?

Whether it's the wife who feels shame because of her husband's infidelity, or the professional who constantly struggles to prove his worth and competence, or the pastor who suffers chronic depression faltering under the heavy weight of ministry, or the boss and/or dad who makes things all about him and his importance in an effort to manage the inadequacy that he secretly has struggled with for most of his life, *they all face the same question that haunts them on a daily basis:*

Am I enough?

Is that wife enough to merit her husband's undivided attention and affection?

Is that professional enough to fill the role and expectations of his employment?

Is that pastor enough to effectively lead his church and meet the needs of his congregation?

Is that boss/dad enough to be recognized for the man and leader he always aspired to be?

Are they enough?

Are you enough?

What's curious about the serpent's tactics in the Garden of Eden when beguiling Eve is that he didn't argue; he didn't bluster or bully; he didn't negotiate, bargain, or bribe. His approach was far more subtle and deviously ingenious.

He just inserted a seed of doubt.

In Genesis we read:

> *"Of course we may eat fruit from the trees in the garden," the woman [Eve] replied. "It's only the fruit from the tree in the middle of the garden that we are not allowed to eat. God said, 'You must not eat it or even touch it; if you do, you will die.'"*

> ***"You won't die!"*** *the serpent replied to the woman. "God knows that your eyes will be opened as soon as you eat it, and you will be like God, knowing both good and evil."*

When Eve heard the serpent's retort, undoubtedly waves of questions flooded her mind.

Questions like:

Can I really trust God?
Does he really want the best for me?
Is he hiding something from me?

And ...

Am I really enough, or can I be even more?

The twist here is that when Eve bit that fruit, she went from "being enough" to "never will be enough" in the blink of an eye. It happened that fast. She went from beautiful to hopelessly broken in less than a second.

Thankfully, God knew this, and that is why he sent us Jesus—because on our own, we never are enough and never will be. But with Jesus, we are more than enough.

The problem is, of course, that in our pride and arrogance, we can't accept this fact, so we continually seek to become the very thing we never can be without God—*enough*. And so doubt floods our minds each day as we continue to ask, *"Am I enough?"* when we all damn well know the answer.

This is irony.
This is life.

This is shame.

Chapter 4

SACRED SEXUALITY

Over the past ten years of working in this area of ministry, I have run into many questions from both men and women. The questions are reasonable, ludicrous, bizarre, and everything that runs the gamut in between. Usually these questions are concerning methods and "keys" to breaking free from unwanted sexual behavior, but often they are related to the topic of sex itself.

Generally speaking, the questions I get about sex fall into one of two categories.

1) I'm having no sex or infrequent sex, so what can I do?

2) What is allowed and not allowed when it comes to sex?

In both these cases, what the person is asking boils down to this: *They want permission.*

Now stop and think about it, but doesn't it seem strange that they would ask permission from someone they don't know about one of the most personal aspects of their lives?

They aren't asking me...

Can I swap out white bread for wheat bread?
Can I buy sneakers that cost more than $100 but really look great?
Can I eat chili even though it makes me fart a lot?
Can I lease my next car despite the payment being a little higher than my comfort level?

No, they are asking someone on the other end of a computer what they can or cannot do when it comes to this most intimate area.

And why?

Because, in my opinion, the mystique and shame we've created around the areas of sex and sexuality are so overwhelming that the only person they feel comfortable talking to about it is someone who's not directly connected to them. Or to put it another way, they are trying to reach out to someone without exposing themselves to unwanted vulnerability.

The problem, of course, is that when we don't feel that we can have these conversations with the people we should be having them with, we end up going down the wrong path or forming unhealthy and inaccurate theologies about one of the most beautiful and spectacular aspects of God's creative design.

Over the years, so much damage has been done to people because of sexual suppression and shame.

Somehow, many people (especially those from a faith background) have grown up believing that sex is kind of a taboo topic, and even though it's OK for marriage, it's almost wrong to pursue for sexual pleasure.

Hear me on this.

Sex is pleasurable, and it's pleasurable for a reason—that's no accident.

We need to stop treating sex and sexuality as if they are dirty words. They aren't. We need to stop acting as if sex is a necessary evil for the continuation of our species. It's not. And we need to celebrate the amazing gift God has given us and not run from it as if it's a wildfire waiting to consume us. It doesn't have to be.

Because when these topics are explored and pursued in an unhealthy manner, they can lead to massive problems and even trauma.

It is possible to acknowledge the pleasure, beauty, and purpose of sex without exploiting or suppressing it. And it's also possible and healthy to openly explore the questions we have around these matters because doing so allows for growth, maturity, and a better understanding of sex and sexuality in their entirety, eliminating the need for disconnected permissions.

Sex Education(less)

One of the aspects of being a pastor that I enjoy most is the bizarre or surprising looks I often get from people when I tell them what I do for a living. I think it's the tattoos that throw them off a bit. But the truth is that I am indeed an ordained pastor.

In fact, at age forty when I felt God calling me into ministry, I went back to school, enrolled in seminary, welcomed more student loan debt, and pursued a master's degree in theological studies, which I did eventually earn. The reason I did so was that I believed I was following a calling, and I should get as much training and preparation as possible. And since I was never formally trained to be a minister, I did what most people do when they want to enter the world of ministry—*I got a degree.*

I have to be honest. Looking back on my education and the cost of it, I'd have to say the return on investment was marginal. Yes, I took some classes I found tremendously informative and helpful, but then there were some required courses that stopped being relevant to me the second the semester wrapped up.

When you look at all the courses many seminarians have to take, you might scratch your head and wonder why they would subject themselves to such an experience. Greek, Hebrew, linguistics—these are just some of the subjects that are typical requirements for any master's-level seminary degree program. But hey, I get it—we want our leaders to be well rounded and thoroughly prepared for the trials and challenges of leading a church or ministry.

I personally was able to avoid the Hebrew and Greek course requirements, but I did take several counseling courses, systematic theology (1 and 2), apologetics, and evangelism.

And through all those classes, books, lectures, and notes, **the one topic strangely absent from any discussion was sex.**

For instance, in theology, I learned all sorts of relatively useless information best fit for theological and philosophical debates sitting around the coffee table, but not much value when it comes to daily life. Yet the one theological topic that apparently no one needed help with was sex and sexuality?

Really? Is it just me, or does that make little to no sense?

Think about it. Men and women attend seminary to better prepare themselves for the task of shepherding and guiding people through the many real-world challenges and difficulties of life, but the one area that creates more brokenness and deeper trauma than almost anything else is practically ignored.

Strange.

I wanted to make sure that this wasn't just unique to my experience, so I did some research and reviewed several master's-level programs from very well-known seminaries, and in almost every case, the degree requirements lacked any sort of training on sex and sexuality.

For instance, if you want a master's of divinity in church ministry in the digital age, of the sixty-three credit hours required, there are zero hours related to sex, sexuality, or internet pornography issues. But Greek and Hebrew?

Yeah—you'll need those courses. It's the same deal if you are seeking a degree in youth and family ministries.

Can you say out of touch? No wonder...

There's so much confusion in the church about sex and sexuality.

We see so little discussion about porn and masturbation.

Youth have trouble embracing the true beauty of God's intent for sexual expression.

Because if those leading them have never been properly educated or equipped to foster discussions in these areas, it's a foregone conclusion that they will lack the needed understanding themselves. There's an old saying, *"Shit rolls downhill."* Guess what—so does ignorance.

Of course, what makes this situation even worse is that public education openly offers its take on sex, but such views are generally focused on the mechanics and gender identification, nothing on its purpose or its role in building true intimacy. And so what we end up with is a generation of people who know a whole lot about intercourse, orgasms, STDs, and gender roles, but little to nothing about God's design for sex and the beauty of its intended purpose.

Favorite Pastime

Before we even can think about approaching the topic of sex in a beneficial and uplifting way, we need to dispel a very common misconception.

Sex is not a fun thing to do that just happens to work best in a marriage situation.

It's not a hobby.
It's not a pastime.
It's not an activity.

No, sex is so much more than the physical act that leads to an orgasm (which admittedly is pretty awesome). Sex was created for marriage, not the other way around, and it serves a very unique purpose.

Recognize that when talking about the relationship a man has with a woman in the context of marriage, we are dealing with a connection that is meant to be so intimate, so personal, and so spiritual that it creates a bond unlike any other relationship we have. This is why in the Bible, God says, *"A man shall leave his father and mother and be joined to his wife, and the two shall become one flesh'; so then they are no longer two, but one flesh. Therefore what God has joined together, let not man separate."* It's also why Jesus uses the picture of a bride and bridegroom when describing his relationship with the church.

Because...

Marriage is unique.
Marriage is intimate.
Marriage is secure.
Marriage is shame free.

Or at least that was the idea.

And so sex serves the purpose of cultivating this unique relationship in way that perfectly represents the ideals of marriage. No other activity on the planet brings two people together in such a way where they are completely vulnerable, completely bare, and completely connected. Consequently, when we start to appreciate the true purpose and meaning behind sex, it is easy to understand how it can so easily go off the rails when pursued in a casual or selfish manner.

Because sex is about bringing two people together, not just about individual pleasure.

What so many men and women fail to appreciate is the holistic nature of sex. Yes, it's a physical act (as is masturbation), but the emotional and spiritual implications of that act are profound. And so when we treat, view, or talk about sex in terms of simple intercourse, we lose sight of the bigger picture, which then inevitably colors our expectations and sexual encounters. It's no wonder there is so much sexual dysfunction in the world.

Imagine if...

We worried about putting gas in our car but forgot about the oil.
We focused on eating proteins but starved ourselves of fats and carbohydrates.
We fed and clothed our kids but never hugged or encouraged them.
We learned to read but never to write.

The results would not be good, because when we have only half the story, the ending never makes sense. And it's the same way with sex. We need to fully appreciate its intended purpose and design to properly navigate the complexities of any sexual experience. Because when we do, things get less confusing and we stop needing to ask for permission to do what we can clearly figure out for ourselves. Additionally, we begin to remove the shame and awkwardness surrounding the topic of sex because we start to see it as a good gift from God, not just some naughty little pastime we occasionally engage in to satisfy our lustful cravings.

Understand that what God designed is beautiful and special. It serves a unique and holy purpose. And when you treat sex with the care and sanctity it deserves, you allow for greater intimacy and a deeper spiritual connection with your spouse while enjoying the pure pleasure sex affords you.

Pure Nonsense

Over the years, one thing that has always stood out to me and others I have talked to outside of Christianity is the church's focus on behavior and clean living. Whether it's deserved or not, the reality is that when most people hear the word "Christian," they think of someone who spends his day concerning himself with making "correct" choices and lecturing others along the way on their need to do the same.

And when it comes to sexual behavior, this is especially true.

Spend any time immersed in evangelical culture, and undoubtedly you will hear the word "purity" come up whenever the topic of sexuality is brought up. Endless books, courses, podcasts, and sermons have been churned out over the years promoting the need for purity and the suppression or denial of sexual desire. Just type in the word "purity" when doing a book search on Amazon, and you'll get over 10,000 results.

The upshot of all this?

A lot of unhelpful advice that doesn't work.

Don't get me wrong—"purity" is not a dirty word. God calls his people to be pure, but reducing the meaning of the word "purity" to a checklist of do's and don'ts misses the bigger picture. And when applying this type of behavior-focused thinking to the concept of "sexual purity," it can prove to be unhelpful and extremely shame-inducing.

Regardless of the original intent, culture's hijacking of the term "purity" has led many to believe that the path to righteous sexuality lies in the choices we make and the ability to say "no." As a result, the purity litmus test often comes down to how we answer questions such as,

> Do I look at porn?
>
> Do I have sex outside of marriage?
>
> Do I masturbate?
>
> Do I lust after or get sexually aroused by other individuals?

This is why when I talk to my kids—or to anyone else, for that matter—about sex and sexuality, I stay away from the term "purity" and favor the term "integrity." Because while looking at porn, masturbation, and sexual promiscuity are not traits that reflect sexual integrity, the absence of these behaviors does not automatically equate to having sexual integrity either.

Sexual integrity is a much broader and deeper term.

Sexual integrity doesn't just focus on behavior. It also factors in intention, motive, consistency, and more. It not only considers our choices, but also the heart with which we make those choices.

In other words, it goes way beyond just a simple list of do's and don'ts.

Sexual integrity allows far more room for grace and movement in our lives because it recognizes that while we may make mistakes and fail occasionally, we can still fully and authentically pursue integrity.

Purity, when understood as it often has been taught, doesn't allow for the same give and take.

The difference between "purity" and "sexual integrity" is much like the difference between the words "spotless" and "clean." If I'm looking for a "spotless" shirt, even a really small spot is a problem, because a spotless shirt literally can't have a spot, no matter what the size. There is no room for grace with the word "spotless" because the definition demands *perfection*.

However, the word "clean" takes into consideration a much larger set of qualities. A clean shirt not only lacks a multitude of stains, but it also smells good, is fresh, and has been recently laundered.

"Spotless" doesn't factor in these concerns.

So you can wear a spotless shirt without it being clean, but on the flip side, you can wear a clean shirt that may *not* necessarily be spotless. Clean does not mean perfect, but it does carry with it a high standard and recognizes that something once dirty has the potential to be brought back to its original pristine state.

Purity not so much because again, pure is pure. There is no margin for error or blemish.

This is why when talking about purity in today's culture, things can get really confusing, because so much focus is placed on one's behavior rather than character. One misstep, one mistake, one questionable decision, and you become damaged goods.

You become impure.

Evidence of this confusion can be seen in how today's youth approaches sex and the notion of virginity. For instance, in a 2012 study focused on oral and anal sex practices among high school youth, they found that of those participants admitting to having oral or anal sex, 86 percent cited preserving virginity as one of their primary reasons for engaging in such acts (as opposed to vaginal sex).[10]

Let that sink in a minute.

In what universe does it make sense that someone would engage in oral or anal sex in order to maintain one's virginity? Let me answer that: **In one where virginity and the forgoing of vaginal penetration is valued greater than ideals we hold when it comes to sex.**

This is why messaging and our understanding concerning sex and sexuality need to transcend rules and boundaries. God is concerned with the heart. Unfortunately, the terms "virginity" and "purity" don't always encapsulate this truth. In fact, such words, if not spoken of in the appropriate context, can be a source of both pride and shame, depending on the individual, rather than an ideal that reflects God's beautiful design.

Sexual Sabotage

Psychology Today[11] describes self-sabotaging behavior as an action that "creates problems in daily life and interferes with long-standing goals." In other words, we create self-sabotaging scenarios when we choose to engage in activities that work against our own good or purposes. When it comes to such things as porn and sexual integrity matters, we can all easily understand how these types of behaviors and choices are damaging and serve as a form of self-sabotage for those who engage in them.

But what if I told you that the sabotaging started way before those individuals ever clicked that mouse for the first time or walked into that first strip club? And what if I told you that we all play a part in setting the stage for those unfortunate scenarios by the *cultural sexualization* we participate in? Let's just address the very large elephant in the room many choose to ignore, because it's uncomfortable and awkward.

Sexualization is (practically speaking) unavoidable, and we all do it.

Sexualization is defined by the *Cambridge Dictionary* as "the act of sexualizing someone or something (i.e., seeing someone or something in sexual terms)." In other words, we sexualize someone when we place value on a person's appearance and sexual appeal above all other characteristics. The problem with sexualizing behavior, of course, is that when we allow ourselves to sexualize someone (including ourselves), we treat that person as an object for others' sexual use rather than recognizing his or her individual capacity, agency, and identity.

In plain terms, we reduce them.

Additionally, cultural sexualization leads to all sorts of social problems and ills such as emotional and self-image problems, self-objectification, an increase in sexually permissive attitudes, the proliferation of pornography, sexual coercion and abuse, and sex trafficking.

That being said, with the rise of the "Me Too" movement and other similar awareness initiatives, sexualization and objectification have become real hot-button issues leading to a general public outcry against such social phenomena. And most of us (especially in the church world) like to think and act as if we don't condone the sexualization that happens on a daily basis with our entertainment and media. Consequently, we complain about sexualized marketing practices and clamor for television programming that doesn't border on soft-core porn.

But we fail to acknowledge that sexualization happens in our own homes and churches on a daily basis. We also fail to recognize that while we should not see other people as solely sexual beings, the reality is that sexuality is part of their being. Or to put it another way, we are more than our sexuality, but we are not detached from our sexuality.

So sexualization is bound to happen.

Right or wrong, good or bad, we live in a culture that will continue to lean on sexualization as an effective way to market, sell, and get noticed. And so, when we shy away from talking about the adverse effects of such things, we commit egregious self-sabotage and set our fellow citizens up for moral failure and sexual compromise.

Here's the truth: We can't have it both ways.

We can't live in a sexualized society and even promote sexualization at times in our speech and actions, and then pretend it doesn't exist and shouldn't impact people negatively.

To do so is extreme hypocrisy at best, and malicious intent at worst.

Consequently, we need to stop spending so much effort on fighting and running from cultural sexualization, and instead, focus on learning how to positively and critically engage with it. Because while in an ideal world there should be some safe spaces where we can enjoy a small reprive from the sexual onslaught, the reality is there are very few, if any, such places.

For instance, in today's modern church culture, while the forms of sexualization may be less obvious, they are still very much present. I can tell you first hand that I've often walked into churches where many young women are wearing pencil skirts tighter and shorter than you'd ever think reasonable, and tops so snug and low cut that they leave little to the imagination.

Then you have pastors who stand up front and talk about their "smoking hot wife" as part of their sermon introduction or a punchline to a joke. Because, apparently, bragging about your wife's high IQ isn't anywhere near as attention grabbing or entertaining. And let's not forget those Christian "leaders" out there who write best-selling books that tell women they should always be available for sex to their husbands (regardless of their own enjoyment) and that failure to do so is a "sin." In fact, one very popular book about male sexual integrity suggested that a wife should be OK with serving as methadone (i.e., a replacement) for their husband's porn addiction.

Listen, I'm no prude.

I don't think that clothes need to be baggy to be acceptable, nor am I an honorary member of the modesty police. The way one chooses to dress never excuses any resulting objectification that may occur. And husband, if you think your wife is "hot," good for you. I hope so.

All that said, the fact remains that sexualization occurs even in our churches, and honestly, we shouldn't be surprised. Again, we are in part sexual beings, and so dressing in ways that draw attention to that fact is to some extent expected. However, when we are finally willing to concede this, then we need to be more vocal about the matters of sex and sexuality in general.

We can't proclaim purity and sexual integrity without acknowledging that there are those among us (a large percentage, incidentally) who struggle in these areas needing help, grace, empathy, and a healthy dose of support. Likewise, we desperately need to start talking about sex and sexuality in healthy ways and incorporating these conversations into the fabric of our communities instead of running from them.

Rather than being sheepish on the matters of sex, we should be bold in our acknowledgement that God created sex, and it is beautiful and enjoyable. It was given to us for the purposes of building intimacy and connection. And when kept within the confines of healthy and holy marriages, sex is highly spiritual and should be celebrated, not shunned. Yes, sex can be a little scary to talk about, but if we can't get past our irrational fears of sex and sexuality, many will continue to struggle in their ignorance and brokenness.

Let's Talk About Sex, Baby

Back in 1990, hip-hop group Salt-N-Pepa released their famous song "Let's Talk About Sex." While a very popular song that hit #13 on the Billboard Hot 100 chart, due to its obvious sex-focused theme, it wasn't exactly a popular choice among the average Christian. And while the song talked about sex and sexuality in a rather shallow one-dimensional way, some of the lyrics were pretty honest and insightful.

> *Let's talk about sex, baby*
> *Let's talk about you and me*
>
> **Let's talk about all the good things**
> **And the bad things that may be**
>
> *Let's talk about sex for now*
> *To the people at home or in the crowd*
> *It keeps coming up anyhow*
> **Don't be coy, avoid, or make void the topic**
> **Cuz that ain't gonna stop it**
>
> *Now we talk about sex on the radio and video shows*
> *Many will know anything goes*
> **Let's tell it how it is, and how it could be**
> **How it was, and of course, how it should be**
>
> *Those who think it's dirty, have a choice*
> *Pick up the needle, press pause, or turn the radio off*

Regardless of the song's overall message, we could learn a thing or two from it. Because the truth is this: **We don't**

talk about sex nearly enough. Not just in church or in our youth groups and/or small groups, but in our homes and in our marriages as well. I can't tell you how many times I've spoken to men who are seemingly unsatisfied with their sex lives, only to find out that they've never shared those same concerns with their spouses. Or if they had, it was only once or twice before they gave up.

Why does this happen?

Primarily because many of us lack a healthy understanding of sex in the first place, and therefore we feel very ill-prepared to tackle these difficult conversations. How does one ask for more sex without looking like a horny dog? How does a wife tell her husband that what he does in the bedroom isn't very enjoyable? How does a young teen ask his parents for a good reason *not to have sex* with the girl he swears he's in love with? The list of awkward and difficult questions goes on and on.

Ultimately, how do we have difficult conversations about sex without hurting feelings, starting arguments, or creating tension and judgment?

The truth is that it's not easy and it never will be. But that doesn't mean we don't do it. However, I do believe that most of the difficulties we run into when discussing sex are because of the way we enter those conversations. In other words, we don't express ourselves in a way that truly reflects our deepest concerns and pains. For instance…

Typically, when an argument over sexual frequency between spouses happens, the conversation looks something like this:

Husband: *Hey, why don't we have sex more?*

Wife: *I don't know. I'm just not always in the mood.*

Husband: *That's the problem—you're never in the mood!*

Wife: *That's not true, but of course you'd say that.*

Husband: *I guess I'm just not good enough for you.*

Wife: *No, not at all. You don't get it.*

Husband: *Get what? You never want to have sex? I have needs, you know.*

Wife: *You can always masturbate like you do anyway.*

Husband: *Typical crap with you ... forget it.*

Wife: *OK, forgotten.*

What comes out of those exchanges? Shame, distrust, anger, and resentment—nothing good. Certainly nothing that will help draw the two together or increase their shared intimacy.

Opportunity missed.

But imagine how this conversation could have gone if they had been brave and thoughtful enough to express their true feelings and desires. Rather than an experience that further fractures their relationship, it could have served as a tremendous growth opportunity. Here's how that exchange could have played out:

> **Husband:** *Hey, I know sometimes you're very tired, but I feel like we don't have sex very often and I miss being with you in that way. Is there something wrong or something I can do differently? I think that lack of physical intimacy isn't the best thing for us.*
>
> **Wife:** *Well, if you want me to be honest with you, too often when you want to have sex, it seems rushed and on your terms. You don't seem overly concerned with my pleasure, and when I am just tired, I feel like you get angry with me. But I do want to have great sex with you.*
>
> **Husband:** *Wow! I'm sorry. That was never my intention. One-way sex is not what I'm after, and if I ever made it feel like I wasn't concerned with your needs, I am sorry. What can I do better?*
>
> **Wife:** *Maybe if we went on a date or spent some quiet time together earlier in the day or evening. More foreplay would be nice, too. I like it when you rub my back. I just don't want to be rushed into hopping into bed.*
>
> **Husband:** *That sounds great. Let's go out this weekend and talk some more over dinner. And then who knows … maybe an awesome back rub, too? Sound like a plan?*

Wife: *Sounds great!*

*Cue Marvin Gaye's "Let's Get It On" instrumental.

Admittedly, this is a simplified version of what a real talk would look like, and chances are it would be several talks like this, not just one. But hopefully you get the idea. The point is we need to spend more time trying to explore our feelings and communicating our real and deepest concerns and less time deflecting so we can just stay comfortably numb.

Because when we engage and openly talk about the challenges we experience rather than retreating from them, we grow in our awareness, emotional intelligence, and understanding, leaving us better prepared for whatever may come next. My wife and I have had these moments ourselves. It's never been easy or comfortable, but we've always come out stronger and better when we've been brave enough to face down the discomfort in the interest of strengthening our relationship.

Ultimately, the answer to your unmet needs and unanswered questions will not be resolved with fear, anger, or ignorance. It will be discovered only through thoughtful engagement and understanding, through a process of commitment to acknowledging "how it is, and how it could be, how it was, and of course, how it should be."

Chapter 5

THE SILENCE THAT KILLS

At face value, it may seem odd that a boy who had two parents and grew up in a Christian home, hardly ever missed church, went to Christian school, attended several Christian summer camps, and was part of various youth groups, grew up to be a raging porn addict.

At face value…

But statistics from multiple studies over the past decade continue to provide evidence that my own story is relatively common as compared with other Christian men. In fact, Barna's research in 2016 reported these numbers:[12]

- 20 percent of youth pastors admit to currently struggling with porn.

- 53 percent of all pastors within the last twelve months have learned that someone they know in ministry struggles with porn.

- 47 percent of Christians say pornography is a major problem in their homes.

- 59 percent of practicing Christian married men have sought a pastor's help for porn use.

And these are statistics based on the assumption that people are actually telling the truth! Not too hard to imagine that the real numbers could be far worse.

But here is the part that makes me scratch my head…

Just 7 percent of pastors say their church has a ministry program for those struggling with porn.

This number, while seemingly illogical, is completely consistent with my experience.

When reflecting on my own life, I can honestly say that throughout all the Sunday sermons, youth group meetings, special speakers, and "Bible" classes I attended, I heard the topic of porn and masturbation talked about less than a few times (and that's being generous).

No wonder we are all such a helpless lot at times.

Sexualized messaging and media assaults young (and old) minds around the clock, and when these experiences create tension and questions for us, no one wants to talk about it or provide any solutions.

Not even our spiritual leaders or communities.

The truth is that the subject of pornography is not an easy one. It's often awkward, uncomfortable, and extremely challenging.

It's not sexy (ironically).

It's not uplifting.

It's not encouraging.

It's not inspiring.

Real talk?

There is no obvious ROI (return on investment) for a church to aggressively tackle this issue because doing so is probably not going to increase giving or put butts in the seats.

In fact, it may have the opposite effect due the pain and discomfort it causes.

I can't tell you how many times I have heard the following when talking to church leaders about their lackluster efforts to help people struggling with porn:

- It's very hard trying to find someone who can lead.

- It's a difficult subject to preach on or talk about on a Sunday.

- It's hard to get anyone to actually respond or participate when we have offered something.

- It requires too much attention when there are other pressing needs.

- I don't have enough expertise to talk about it knowledgeably.

And while all of these are very reasonable and legitimate objections, it doesn't mean we avoid the real challenges of doing so, because when we refuse to engage in these conversations, we fuel the shame that surrounds them.

We have to do more.

We have to do better.

And while this means we will certainly come up against setbacks and frustrations, if we push through the pain and discomfort, we can all experience a tremendous breakthrough.

I understand it's very easy to be a critic when you don't have to do the job.

But there needs to be a change.

Because unlike some who say the church would just be better to back out of this stuff completely, I believe in the calling of the church and its vital role in restoring a broken world.

Jesus called us to be salt and light all the time, not just when it's easy or convenient.

The Church Bagman

Anyone who has watched an episode of *The Wire* has probably heard the terms dealer, pusher, corner boy, and bagman, all of which refer to people who sell drugs on the local level, usually while standing on the corner trying to look inconspicuous. After all, you can't really hold up a sign drawing attention to your services when in that line of "work."

And while I never sold drugs or stood on a street corner peddling narcotics, I kinda know what it feels like to be that guy.

Let me explain...

When the story came out in the paper about my story, my work with XXXchurch, and the local recovery group I was hosting, word sort of got out in my church. Suddenly, I became the "church porn guy," and as a result, I frequently would have men approach me in the church about their struggles because they knew I was a safe place.

Except they never approached me in an open setting. They never brought it up in the midst of our weekly small group or over coffee near the "greeter" station in the church foyer.

No, typically they'd sheepishly pull me aside when no one was around, and the ensuing conversation would go something like this:

> *Hey Carl.*
> *Hey man, what's up?*

> *Can we talk?*

At this point, my wife would casually walk away with our kids, knowing what was coming next.

> *Sure, whatcha got?*

> *Can we go over there to talk?* (pointing around a corner or curtain)

> *Yeah, for sure.*

Once we both arrived at the designated "out of the way" spot in the church, I'd then get something like…

> *Hey, so I struggle with porn, and I know you work with guys that do, so I figured **you'd be a safe person to talk to.** Do you have any advice? I really need some help.*

Did you catch that?

I was a safe person to talk to—a safe person, as opposed to all the other "unsafe" people in the church?!?

And what made me safe?

Was it the fact that these guys knew when they unloaded their dark secrets on me, I wouldn't heap a ton of shame on them as a reward for their honesty and transparency?

Was it because I hosted a weekly porn-focused recovery group in my home while our church never bothered to do the same?

Was it because I was willing to share my story in a local paper, so they felt confident they could share their story with me?

Maybe it was all of this?

Regardless, there I was, a guy trying to help other guys out of their sexual brokenness, only to find myself operating in the shadows because church wasn't seen as a safe enough place to come clean about these things.

Right or wrong, good or bad, this was the case. And sadly, it's a far too common scenario I see playing out in many churches today. The hard reality is that as long as we continue to treat sex and porn like taboo matters only fit for the most private of conversations, we will struggle to convince those struggling in these areas that the church is a safe haven for them to turn to for help.

Recognize when we remain silent on the matters of sex, porn, and masturbation, we send a message that those topics aren't welcomed for conversation so "just keep it to yourself." Almost nothing is harder for a person struggling with sexual shame than when he feels that his real-world concerns are of absolutely no concern to you.

Except when we talk about these struggles in a condemning, condescending, and generally unhelpful manner.

Anti-Porn Alienation

I have a confession to make. I am not "anti-porn" or "against porn."

I know… *"Wait, what?!?! Did I hear that right?"*

That's right. I said it. I'm not.

But I'm also not "pro-porn" or "for porn" either. And no, that's not my clever way of refusing to take a stand. It's just that those are two entirely different positions that connote two entirely different mindsets.

I certainly don't believe that porn is good, helpful, or healthy. In fact, I don't feel that porn has any redeeming value whatsoever. But I also don't believe that porn is to blame for all the sexual brokenness we see in our world today.

Porn is simply an option. It's not a requirement. No one is forced to consume or pursue pornography. It's just there, like it or not.

But in religious circles, the common approach to addressing problems like porn addiction and the sex industry as a whole is to "FIGHT IT" and to demonize it. Here are just a few of the sentiments I've run into often coming from religious folk and organizations:

> Porn kills your relationship with God.

> Porn kills love.

> Porn is rape education.

> Porn normalizes rape culture.

And while I understand the logic behind this messaging, I feel this type of "anti-porn" agenda is problematic because it creates some unintended consequences that are difficult to deny or avoid.

Such as crushing shame.

Like it or not, the truth is when we completely demonize a behavior or industry, we unintentionally send the message that those engaging in these things are to be demonized as well, and rather than inviting them into a healthy dialogue, we shut down the dialogue altogether.

Why?

Because when I hear you say, "I'm against this," I also hear "I'm against you."

The reality is, when one engages in behavior that is seen as vile or terribly wrong vs. just simply unhealthy, then the collateral shame the person feels is thick and will keep them from opening up about this stuff or seeking help to avoid public disgrace.

And when we as a society or church rather choose to keep ringing the same ol' "This is really bad" bell without the willingness to talk about these things in the open, we further affirm the shameful nature of those behavior choices.

Moral Rhetoric

Whether it is porn, masturbation, or any other forms of "sexual sin," one of the most complicating factors that muddies the water around healthy dialogue is the "morality" of it all. After all, if we are talking about compulsive eating, poor financial mismanagement, workaholism, or any other number of dysfunctional behaviors, it's usually a matter of how much is too much.

A little fast food is evidence that you don't always stick to your diet.
A little overspending says you enjoy spoiling yourself.
A little too much focus on work identifies you as a go-getter.

But a little porn, masturbation, or infidelity just means you are immoral.

And theologically speaking, there is no argument to that fact. Consequently, when leaders from a faith-based background tackle these topics, they tend to address these behaviors more from a morality or purity police perspective than with a critical mind and a helping hand.

For example…

Not too far back, a friend of mine forwarded a message that his pastor had preached about porn. My friends do this often because I'm one of the few (if not only) "porn" pastors they know.

Now, before I say anything else, let me just state that it's very commendable that this pastor addressed such a touchy issue so directly AND from the pulpit on a Sunday morning. But the sermon was predictable and not very helpful.

The basic outline went something like this:

1) Porn is bad and a sin.

2) It's a serious problem.

3) If you look at it, you have a serious problem.

4) Go get some help.

5) Let's pray.

No suggestion on where to get help. No direction or guidance. No offer of assistance. None of that. Just … here's the problem. You have a problem. Now go fix the problem. Good luck.

And we wonder why so many people in today's church stay stuck and clueless when it comes to getting the help they need.

We need to understand that if the church is going to do a better job at addressing the needs of the sexually broken and reducing the shame that surrounds those struggles, we must focus less on purity and more on pain.

At the end of the day, the real issue behind sexual brokenness is not the morality of choices we make, but the reasons we make those choices in the first place. We need to stop treating hurting people as if they are children who can't behave themselves and more like the wounded souls they really are.

We need to open up our arms and hearts instead of shaking our heads and pointing fingers.

Recognize that morality and purity are not bad words. But if we want to experience the benefits of a "moral" life, we must be willing to talk about the pain of living in the first place.

As St. Augustine once said, the church is "a hospital for sinners, not a museum for saints." We need to adopt this type of healing mindset even more so when offering help and care to the sexually broken who carry around some of the deepest wounds you can imagine.

This means extending love and grace not only to our church family, but also to its leadership.

Ecclesiastic Cannibalism

A few years ago I received a call from a man who was an elder at a church in Texas. He called me because he had a situation and wanted some advice. The "situation" was this…

One of their youth ministers had (suddenly) incurred a large data charge on his church-paid mobile phone line. When the man was confronted with this and asked for a justification for the large data usage, he confessed that he had been struggling with online porn.

Shoe dropped.

This elder was looking for some advice on what to do with the young pastor, specifically in terms of his employment.

Now, before I tell you what I said, let me fill you in on a pretty important detail. As it turned out, this youth pastor had previously approached his senior pastor about his struggle two years prior to this incident. When he did this, his senior pastor essentially told him to just work on it and "get better."

No advice.

No care.

No accountability or plan.

Just, well, stop doing it.

Now back to our story…

So I told the elder that since this guy had previously sought help, and then was honest when he was confronted about this issue, they probably shouldn't fire him but maybe reassign him for the time being and **put him on a short leash**. Additionally, they should provide some good accountability and get him some resources, so they could walk him through the process of recovery and restoration.

The man thanked me for my time, wrote down some resources and links I recommended, and hung up.

A couple weeks later, I followed up with this guy to see what had happened.

Did they take my advice?
Did they find him some help?

Did they care for him when he needed it most?

Nope. They fired him.

Which leads me to this point.

It is our own lack of grace when it comes to leadership that creates environments where perfection is expected and transparency is discouraged. And so, when we abandon and readily jettison our own leaders whenever they make a mistake, need help, and are honest about that fact, it's unlikely those same leaders will foster cultures where open conversations about such issues as porn, fidelity, and integrity are encouraged.

In fact, the opposite often happens. We get leaders who blithely ignore these matters or, worse yet, cover them up when there is a moral failure, leading to scandals and even long-term abuse.

How many times in the past few years have we seen the horrific downfall of celebrity-like Christian leaders due to their sexual brokenness and compromise?

How many times have we heard the cries of those victims these leaders deeply hurt?

Too many.

Understand that when a leader fails to seek accountability for their indiscretions, they should be removed. Not simply because of what they did, but because of their unwillingness to pursue genuine repentance reflects a spirit of pride and self-deceit, going against the biblical guidelines for church leadership (Titus 1:5–9).

There is no question that leadership is a privilege and carries with it expectations and standards. But leaders are still human, last time I checked.

And when they are willing to seek accountability for their decisions, when their failures are "brought" and not "caught," when they express repentance and seek healing, our response should not be to roast them on a fire, but to seek to help them through a corrective and restorative process characterized by love and grace (Galatians 6:1).

Ultimately, it falls on our leaders to lead and move church culture in the direction it needs to go. It's on them to create places of safety, grace, and encouragement and to set the example for the rest of us of what it means to live with a sense of transparency, vulnerability, and freedom from shame.

But it's on us to communicate to our leaders that we want to be that place for them as well. And until we stop eating our own when they fail or show signs of weakness, don't expect much to change.

It Takes a Village to Blame

Ready for something that's going to sting a bit?

The "church" is more than just a building, an organization, and its leaders. The church is us. In plain terms, the reason the church is not doing enough when it comes to destroying the strongholds of shame around sex, porn, and masturbation is because **we are not doing enough.**

Sure, it's easy to throw the organizational church and its leaders under the bus since it's clear they've dropped the ball on these complex and difficult matters (or at least that appears to be the general consensus).

But when we do this, we need to jump in front of that bus also.

Because the leaders we condemn are just representatives of what the larger consensus demands.

In other words, we asked for this.

One thing that has always bothered me about the American church is its marriage to the "American dream." We all love the idea of the American dream, but so much of that dream rubs against the ideals of the Kingdom Jesus preached about, such as its obsession with excessive consumerism.

We are all consumers.

This means that we take rather than give, and we want to be served without having to serve. And then we bring that consumer mindset into our "churches."

This is why you see so much focus in modern evangelicalism on the production, on slick programs, on sharp trendy dressed preachers, on fancy lights and fog machines (side note: please lose the fog machines—that stopped being cool twenty years ago), and on topics that are "relevant" yet not too challenging.

This is also why for every person out there who is clamoring for more help and conversation around the issues of sex, porn, and masturbation, there are dozens of people who would rather just keep quiet about these topics because they create awkwardness, discomfort, and yes, shame.

We claim we want more authenticity and transparency in the church, but do we really? Are we ready for what that looks like?

Of course not.

Because most of us would rather be entertained than be made to feel uncomfortable. We want a little honesty and transparency, but not too much. We want community and friendship, but without the messiness that brings.

Yes, we need to push our churches to be more bold and aggressive in how they tackle porn, masturbation, and sex; but we also need the integrity to push ourselves. We need to lead our leaders to a better way of leading us, because when we don't, our resounding silence encourages their apathy.

We all need to understand and accept that change can happen only if we are in this together.

The hurting and the healer.
The churchgoer and the church leader.

It takes all of us to break the silence and defeat the shame.

Chapter 6

ANTI-SOCIAL MEDIA MALAISE

Back when I was a kid, I did some really stupid things. I think that's just part of growing up, to be honest. And while I had more than my fair share of ignorant moments or embarrassing mishaps, all in all, my life maintained a certain trajectory because the damage I inflicted on others and/or on myself was contained.

Unfortunately, in today's social media–saturated world, the way things work when it comes to our expressions and decisions has changed significantly. What once was a dumb picture someone took when intoxicated or an ill-conceived thought expressed in anger can now be a career-ending blunder that escalates out of control in the span of only a few minutes.

Between mobile phone technology, the widespread access of internet connectivity, and most significantly, the plethora of social media platforms out there, we find ourselves living in a world where we all are digitally connected with just a few taps of a keypad.

Here are some crazy statistics as it pertains to our collective use of social media:

As of 2021...

- There are 3.78 billion social media users worldwide (that's roughly half of the global population).

- The average user wastes,—I mean spends—2.5 hours a day on social media.

- Almost 50 percent of consumers rely on social media "influencers" for recommendations.

- Roughly 80 percent of those ages 18–64 use social media.

Social media has changed the social landscape for almost everyone. *But not necessarily for the better.*

Don't misunderstand me.

The innovation of social media has revolutionized the way we market, connect, and share life experiences with each other. Because of social media, we can get the latest "news" in seconds; we have endless sources of entertainment at our fingertips, courtesy of dancing dogs and water-skiing squirrels; and we have the ability to spread our positive and impactful message to millions of people without spending a red cent or having an established audience.

The reality is that in today's social media world, anyone can be heard and get noticed.

The downside to this? Anyone can be heard and get noticed.

And so, while our capacity to communicate and connect has exponentially increased through the power of social media, so has our ability to both cast and experience shame, making our digital social experiences, well ... not so social after all.

The Comparison Trap

One of the most unique and appealing aspects of social media is that it allows us the ability to share our experiences and great moments with everyone. After all, what's better than enjoying a delicious meal than doing it in front of your five thousand-plus "friends"?

Enjoying a delicious taco with a side of homemade guacamole?

Snap a pic and post.

Captivated by an amazing sunset while on vacation?

Snap a pic and post.

Ready to drink a craft brew that has a 4.7 rating on Untappd?

Snap a pic and post.

About to head out for a needed date night with your beloved spouse?

You guessed it. Snap a pic and post.

And while sharing all your awesome moments in life, making everyone following you green with envy, may sound super appealing (and a bit narcissistic), there's a huge downside to all that cyber bragging.

It fuels social comparison that leads to social anxiety, lower self-esteem, and shame.

See, when I was a kid, keeping up with the Joneses only meant comparing your status and perks to a few neighbors, thus keeping the circle of dissatisfaction limited to a small group of individuals. Plus, the indicators of social and financial success were far more basic and easy to evaluate:

- How big is their house and how many cars do they own?

- Do they have a good job?

- How are their kids with sports and academics?

- How many friends show up when they throw a party?

But these days, the Joneses can be any and every person we follow or interact with on social media. And the metrics we now measure to determine social status, popularity, and success are far more nuanced:

- How many restaurants did they visit last month?

- How many followers and friends do they have?

- How many views and likes do their posts get?

- How many "friends" are tagged in their last comment or pic?

Consequently, as we aimlessly scroll through our feeds searching for funny cat memes to reshare, we're constantly reminded of how much we are apparently missing out on. And while a little social media envy may sound harmless enough, the reality is that it creates tangible psychological distress for many.

In a 2020 survey of Instagram users, researchers noted the following:

> *Our results … showed that social comparison increased one's social anxiety. Social media users often compare themselves with others' appearance, ability, popularity, and social skills. Such comparisons trigger strong psychological responses, particularly when others selectively present more positive information. … Exposure to these idealized images of others can activate negative emotions, contributing to poor psychological well-being such as social anxiety [and] decreased self-esteem.*[13]

In other words, what this survey discovered was that when Instagram users were exposed to photos and posts presenting positive and even idealized portrayals of others in their circles, the resulting social comparison often led to shameful feelings about themselves. And, if I'm being honest, I've fallen into this same comparison trap at times myself, both personally and professionally.

But the crazy thing is that often what we are comparing ourselves to is a fabricated or filtered presentation of reality.

Men and women share cropped and even retouched photos of themselves after a dozen attempts to get just the right shot.

Couples post messages to each other of undying affection below a picture of them at the newest restaurant in town just hours after a huge blowout.

Celebrities share inspirational video messages to their hordes of followers, moments after an emotional breakdown.

And people share images of their latest, greatest purchase or vacation accompanied by hashtags that reflect their "baller" lifestyle, but they leave out any mention of the massive credit card debt they just incurred in the process.

Meanwhile, we sit there wondering why our very real, average, and untouched lives seem to come up so short of what we see others claiming to enjoy.

The truth is that our reality will almost never live up to what we see on social media. But the negative feelings we experience as a result of these comparative exercises are undeniable and impactful. And when we already carry around with us a mountain of guilt and shame from our poor choices or sexual struggles, the natural assumption is that we are missing out on the good life others are enjoying because we don't deserve it and very likely never will.

The Masses Are Asses

When I was a kid, my dad had a saying: *"The masses are asses."*

I know, not very nice...

But while that statement is rather condemning and not very compassionate or love centric, there is a degree of truth to it in that groups will do the wrong thing more often than we care to admit if such action is needed in the interest of conformity. In fact, this was the subject of interest in a series of studies conducted by social psychologist Solomon Asch of Swarthmore College in the 1950s called the Asch Conformity Experiments.

I won't bore you with all the details of the tests themselves, but using flashcards, participants were asked to be part of a group "vision test." Each time, all but one of the participants were working for Asch.

The purpose was to see if the real participant(s) would conform to the obviously wrong answers of the group and change their answer to respond in the same way, despite it being wrong.

In the end, Dr. Asch found that when surrounded by individuals all giving an incorrect answer, participants provided an incorrect response as well 32 percent of the time. That may not sound significant **until you recognize that when there was no pressure to conform, participants provided incorrect answers only 2.8 percent of the time.**[14]

What's the takeaway here?

Simple.

Dr Asch's experiment shows the power of a group when it comes to encouraging conformity. And in today's world, our social media network is about as big a group as you can ask for.

Given this understanding, it's easy to see why so many people will post some of the most hateful, insulting, shameful, and just flat-out insane things you can imagine: because they want to fit in with the social norm of "their group" and/or convince others to conform to that way of thinking.

Social media would have you believe that it's all about individuality and positive expression. But nothing could be further from the truth. Whatever the original intent, in today's culture, social media is more about conformity and pushing agendas than anything else.

Honestly, unless you are posting a family pic or the latest apple pie recipe you found on Pinterest, there is a better than average chance you'll get some sort of negative feedback when you even dare to offer an opinion that's just a little on the provocative side. Because while your "group" may say it encourages free speech and thought, it does so only if what you say or think fits in with *their* cultural norm.

And when we dare to step outside the group and pose an alternate viewpoint? We get met with an avalanche of criticism and personal attacks.

Weapons of Mass Consumption

Although the idea of social media started off as an entertaining way to share and connect with others, it has devolved into a frequently toxic wasteland of weaponized shame. Maybe that sounds harsh, but it doesn't take much scrolling through one's feeds to see how many posts are from people arguing, posturing, and condemning rather than just simply sharing life experiences.

It's sad, but you can easily tell who possesses some level of social awareness and ability to think critically from the masses who just rather post, share, and repost whatever best fits their agenda or the narrative they buy into.

Witness comments like…

> *If you're not with us, you're against us.*
> *Do you have the guts to repost this?*
> *Can I get a like if you agree?*
> *Copy and paste if you aren't too ashamed.*

It's similar to the old chain letters or direct messages that try to guilt you into forwarding them to someone else you know, signaling that you have way too much time on your hands and annoying that person in the process. Ridiculous for sure, but pretty common nevertheless.

In 2020 and 2021, these types of shame-casting messages have never been more prevalent.

Between politics, COVID, vaccination policies, and racial injustice, I've never witnessed more hate, divisiveness, and condemnation in my life, sometimes from people who I once thought were sane and reasonable!

And why? Because...

We feel the need to be on the right side.
We would rather have conformity than healthy dialogue.
We fear rejection and need acceptance.

And quite honestly, we feel threatened when asked to reexamine our values and beliefs.

It would be nice to think that this type of poor online behavior is common only with the insane minority. But alas, this is not so. Politicians, athletes, celebrities, and media personalities all jump into the toxic fray without hesitation. And so what happens?

We grab our megaphones and join the long parade of shame that our leaders began.

And I'll admit it. I've blasted people on social media myself, trying to keep my criticisms focused on public personalities, politicians, or brands that just plain ol' suck when it comes to customer service. But where it can go real south real quick is when we allow our criticisms of a person's actions, stances, policies, or performance drift into an attack on one's character.

Realize that there's nothing wrong with a healthy disagreement, and sometimes a stern call to the carpet is appropriate, such as when dealing with a politician who's not adequately answering the expectations of his or her office.

But when we make judgments on a person's values and/or moral fiber based on a difference of opinion or a disappointing performance, we move from critical observer to mudslinger. And unfortunately, when it comes to social media, mudslinging is very much in style.

Compounding the Shame

Like many things in life, the value of social media comes down to how it's used. When we treat these platforms and tools as a harmless way to connect and be entertained, they can add a small amount of enrichment to our lives. But when we squander away our day scrolling, posting, condemning, and validating, we mitigate any value social media provides, and in fact, we rob ourselves of enjoyment, satisfaction, and self-worth through our unhealthy social comparisons.

Judith White, teaching professor of management at the University of Illinois who holds a Ph.D. in social psychology, stated it this way:

> *Social comparison may result in one believing that external conditions or socially approved benchmarks are more important than internal and personal traits. As one perceives his or her inherent characteristics to be less important in gaining social recognition, the sense of self-esteem will be lowered.*[15]

With this understanding, it is easy to see why so many people jump on board the shame train and fall in line with their group's expectations rather than thinking and deciding for themselves. Any risk of being seen as a nonconformist brings with it potential rejection and/or disapproval, which threatens their fragile sense of self-worth and identity.

What does this mean when we put all that together?

When people see themselves as different from their group's norm, they are more likely to hold a negative evaluation of themselves. This serves as a catalyst to make changes that follow the expectations and values of their identified group, preserving their place in that group.[16]

The result of all this is that individuals who struggle already with acceptance and identity, due to their struggles with matters of sex and sexuality, compound the shame they feel because it further strengthens the misguided lie they've been telling themselves for years:

They don't belong.

Understand that so much about porn use and other unwanted sexual behaviors stems from a person's innate need to belong and be connected. And the reason so many choose to quietly dwell in the shame of their choices is because they can't risk more abandonment, more shame, and more loss. And so in an online world saturated with pretty happy people, unreal life experiences, and guilt-driven agendas, the logical choice becomes the only choice in the face of uncertain acceptance.

Just keep quiet and fit in.

See, while millions of people each day are strategically sharing carefully curated moments of their life like a quasi–"best of" highlight reel, very few people are talking about…

How they blew it and looked at porn or masturbated again.
How things went at their last support and recovery group meeting.
How the sex in their marriage has dried up and their marriage sucks.
How they feel alone and stuck in their sexual addictions.

Because that wouldn't be normal.

And to be honest, it wouldn't be appropriate.

Because the world of social media isn't real and it's often very unhealthy. It's a place filled with individuals who would rather maintain the status quo than upset the proverbial apple cart of those who rather just stay numb and blissfully unaware of life's hard realities. And while social media promises the possibility of endless connection, it can't deliver what we all need—real intimacy.

The type of intimate and unfiltered sharing that we all need to pursue can't be found on Facebook, Instagram, or any of the other dozen platforms where people can waste away their lives. It needs to be done within the context of authentic relationships. And the only thing that stands in the way of that is us and the absurdly high value we place on our privacy.

Chapter 7

THE PRIVACY MYTH

"*It's none of your business.*"

This was a common phrase I heard from my dad over the years growing up and when I worked with him at our family's insurance agency. It didn't matter who was asking—a family member, business partner, or even myself at times. If information was to be had, my father's most typical response was to deflect or remain vague, and when pressed for an answer, he replied with the inevitable *"It's none of your business."*

There were, of course, some occasions when his resistance to divulging information made a degree of sense. Then there were many times when it just seemed arbitrary or even completely unnecessary.

For instance...

When I worked at the insurance agency, we would have insurance company field reps come in every so often to complete an agency review. This would entail going over our production numbers, claims volume, and other information that the carrier wanted to properly evaluate our continued viability as an agent and one of their representatives.

Part of this process included answering questions about our overall agency size and standing with other companies we represented.

Typically, when we did these Q&A sessions, it would be me, my father, and our field rep in a conference room or over lunch. And every time, it was a bit of a painful experience for all of us, because when asked pretty straightforward questions about numbers and dollars, my dad's answers were usually evasive, nonspecific, and even just plain old inaccurate:

> 650,000 equated to "a little under one million."
>
> Six or seven companies became "around a dozen."
>
> One million and one dollar became "between one and two million."
>
> 5–6K in new business translated to "We just wrote around 10K in new policies."

And when asked to nail down a specific answer? Then would come the oh so predictable *"I'm not telling you that"* or *"It's none of your business."*

After these awkward and teeth-grinding sessions, I would often ask my father why he was so coy with his answers. After all, these were, in theory, our business "partners" who were just trying to do their job and keep things copacetic. He would reply that the less they knew, the better, because they wouldn't be able to use that information against us in the future.

Against us? Seems a little paranoid, you might think. But for my father, this was the logical assumption.

The more people know about you, the more they can hurt you, and therefore, the more vulnerable you make yourself.

Privacy was, and is still to this day, something my dad values highly and unfortunately, he's not alone. We all live in a privacy-obsessed culture because the prevailing sentiment is that the more privacy we have, the safer we are. And the safer we are, the less we have to worry about getting hurt.

Unfortunately, what many don't realize is that privacy does not equate to safety. And when we live in such a guarded manner, often we end up doing the very opposite. We put ourselves at a considerably greater risk.

Safety that Hurts

According to a 2021 report by Risk Based Security, in 2020 there were over 3,932 cases of data breaches, exposing over 37 billion records of personal information. That's right, not a typo—37 BILLION!

More than twice the records that had been exposed just one year prior.[17]

With hackers and scammers around every digital corner, it is no wonder that we have become a rather paranoid society when it comes to releasing any personal information. After all, there's no telling whose hands that information could fall into.

In fact, social media experts will tell you to remove all sorts of personal information from your online profiles and lock down your privacy settings in the interest of keeping you "safe" from identity thieves, predators, or just nosy neighbors.

And while all this logically leads us to associating "safety" with "privacy" or secrecy, the truth is they are not the same thing.

Yes, we should maintain "privacy" when it comes to sensitive information such as social security numbers, bank account numbers, medical information, and the like. However, what we often fail to understand is that just because something is sensitive due to its painful, personal, or shameful nature does not mean it needs to be kept private. **In fact, doing so can lead to disastrous consequences.**

Such as our struggles with matters of a sexual nature.

You see, one thing that gives porn addiction and sexual struggles such power in our lives is its secretive nature. We incorrectly think that if we keep our problems and bad choices secret, we won't be found out, and therefore we won't have to deal with the fallout and shame.

But when we buy into that lie, we allow these problems to snowball and grow, leading to horrible repercussions. Ironically, what we choose to keep private or secret in the interest of our "safety" ends up being the very stuff that proves to be our undoing.

See, while the idea of being transparent about our sexual struggles may seem "sensitive," distasteful, uncomfortable, and unsafe, inviting others into our struggles can be one of the best things we can do when it comes to maintaining or regaining our sexual integrity, wholeness, and believe it or not, *safety*.

The Bible echoes this sentiment when it says, *"Two people are better off than one, for they can help each other succeed. If one person falls, the other can reach out and help. But someone who falls alone is in real trouble."*

Real trouble...

Can it be any clearer? Not "some trouble" or a "little trouble" or even "may be in real trouble." No, when we do life as a solo venture, we are headed for ruin and harm, plain and simple. Because when you don't have people in your life that you can confide in and be transparent with (especially when it comes to your sexual struggles), you are destined for compromise.

Transparency allows others into our lives and gives them permission to speak truth into our circumstances. It provides an avenue for authentic sharing, true encouragement, and the sharpening of one another's minds. It allows us to step out from the shadows and divorce ourselves from the shame we feel.

The reality is that a colossal moral failure is always preceded by a series of subtle bad decisions that were left unchecked. However, when we practice a lifestyle of transparency, our community can draw attention to those things and help get us back on course before we drive off the road and into a ditch.

Transparency and accountability function as a lifeline we can grab onto when sliding down the slippery slope of compromise. But when we keep our decision-making and struggles private in the interest of "safety" and avoiding shame, we head down a long road of regret, pain, and isolation.

Sex Talk in a Small Group

Years ago, I was part of a small group that met at a friend's house semi-weekly. The church we attended had started assigning people to various small groups as a way to foster community, and by "foster," I think they meant "force." None of the people we were friends with at our church wanted to be "assigned" to some random group, especially my wife and me, so we asked if we could all meet as a self-formed group. The church agreed and left it to us to choose a "leader" for the group.

The first week we met, we discussed who should lead the group conversations as its de facto leader or facilitator. Everyone went round the room throwing out names, and for some reason, mine kept coming up as the "ideal" choice. Finally, they asked me if I'd be willing to lead our discussions and I agreed, but I warned them that if I was leading, I wanted to make sure we kept the group as real and raw as possible, so we could strive for real growth and connection.

Everyone thought that sounded good and echoed my sentiment that they too wanted an authentic group and not just another typical church small group experience where we were content to throw around spiritual pleasantries over danishes and coffee.

We soon started meeting regularly, and everything was great. Most of us tried to be really honest about what was going on in our lives and families whenever we met as I kept trying to push all of us more and more outside of our comfort zones.

And then I pushed too far…

One week, I mentioned that in a book I had read recently on accountability, the author (a pastor and ministry leader) shared how in a group he had been part of with other male leaders and pastors, they started making it a point to report when the last time they had sex with their spouse as part of their weekly sharing.

The idea behind this rather awkward segment of group participation was that infrequent or absent sex in a marriage was often a red flag for other issues. The author then went on to reveal that shortly after incorporating this practice, it didn't take very long for the group to break up because most of the guys in the group didn't want to talk about something they saw as extremely personal, and in some cases, plain ol' embarrassing.

Judging by the look of shock in our group, I should have known better and stopped there. But I didn't. And so I went on to suggest we do the same thing since we were all married couples, and in theory, we were there to be real and authentic about all aspects of our lives, so we could better help each other stay on track.

The reaction to that suggestion was complete disgust and shock.

> *Why would I ever recommend such a thing?*
> *What was wrong with me, thinking that was a good idea?*
> *Had I lost my mind?*
> *Didn't I realize that the frequency of sex between spouses was no one's business but theirs?*
> *Was I some sort of weirdo?*
> *Obviously, everyone here was happily married.*

Thankfully, that ill-conceived suggestion was not the end of our meeting as a group. But it did tell me one thing…

Our group wanted honesty and complete transparency only if it didn't bring personal discomfort.

Now, if the story ended there, you too might think I just lost my mind temporarily, but there is more. After meeting for about a year, one day a woman in the group who my wife had grown rather close to came to us in tears. She unloaded on both of us about how her marriage was in shambles, her husband didn't really seem to love her, and how even though she wanted their marriage to thrive, he was completely disinterested and didn't want to invest any effort.

After a lot of crying and sobbing, I agreed to meet with the guy one-on-one in an effort to try to foster some sort of reconciliation and hopefully get both spouses on the same page. However, when we got together to talk, he seemed clueless about the whole matter and said that, if anything, she seemed distant and uninterested in him and the marriage as of late.

Things didn't add up.

Until about a month later, when it came out that she was having an affair (with someone I coincidentally knew) and was just looking for a way out. When confronted, she denied that was the case and said it was just a little emotional involvement that went too far.

At that point, it got really messy.

The wife stopped talking to both of us and one of the other families in our group. The husband kept talking to everyone because he just wanted some answers. And the trust between all of us had been irreparably broken.

Eventually, our "authentic" small group disintegrated completely. And despite my wife's best attempts to patch things up with her friend, they never mended the relationship.

Granted, even if we had agreed to talk about our sex lives as a group, that would not have guaranteed us uncovering the issues in their marriage before it got too bad. But the unwillingness and complete disgust expressed for wanting to go there helped set the stage for the unfortunate conclusion to this story.

In the end, no one in our little tribe really wanted to be fully transparent and honest—they just wanted to pretend as if they did.

No doubt that couple had some serious difficulty going on in their lives.
No doubt they felt some shame and embarrassment about their situation.
No doubt the burden they were each carrying alone felt crushing at times.

But ultimately, their attempts to maintain privacy about the realities of their marriage led to a broken situation and even more broken relationships. And this, unfortunately, is how it usually turns out when we avoid uncomfortable conversations and the shame that ensues by remaining secretive about our pain, struggles, and life choices.

The Shameful Pursuit

We offer a free e-course on our websites called the 10 Day Freedom from Porn Action Plan. Thousands of people have done this course, which follows more of a "do-it-yourself" and at your own pace format. But one time we decided to try something new and offer it as a group challenge where a group of men would start the course at the same time, sharing their experiences and thoughts along the way via a private Facebook group we had set up.

It sounded like a great idea to me because by doing this, we would not only educate guys, but we would also come alongside them and support them during the challenge. However, to make this experience more appealing, we rebranded it the 10 Day Sexual Integrity Challenge rather than using the word "porn," avoiding the stigmas associated with being a "porn addict."

Between the rebranding move and the few ads we ran, we ended up netting a little over 300 signups. Not amazing, but not horrendous.

As we approached the official beginning of the challenge, I felt my anticipation begin to ramp up. Most of my excitement was centered on the private group we had set up and the prospect of seeing that many guys working together toward a common goal of freedom and integrity.

Would all 300 men join our private group?
Would they embrace the idea of working together?
Would we see an inspirational collaborative effort unfold during the course of this experiment?

Not really...

The challenge ran two weeks. But by the end of this experiment, less than 100 men joined the private Facebook group. And truth be told, that would have been OK, except less than 15 guys made a single post during the entire length of the challenge.

What was the disconnect?

Why was participation in this challenge so uncomfortable? What were these guys so worried about that they couldn't share even a single thought, encouragement, or even prayer request among a group of men, who in theory, were all there to do the same thing and achieve the same purpose—live a life of integrity?

This was a noble pursuit.

Yet something was off. Somehow going after this very good and virtuous goal was a source of shame and embarrassment for many of the guys who participated.

A couple of weeks after the challenge wrapped up, I talked to a friend of mine who had done the challenge, too. I relayed some of the frustrations I was feeling at the lack of engagement I witnessed. That's when he shared that a couple of his friends had also joined the effort. He went on to say how much they enjoyed the materials we had given them and the experience of it all, *minus the private group.*

I asked him what the issue was with the group. What didn't they like? He replied that he had spoken with one guy in particular, and in that man's words, *"The whole sharing thing was too weird. I'd talk about these things [sex, porn, masturbation] with maybe a couple really close friends, but with a bunch of dudes I don't know? No thanks. That's kinda private."*

There it was.

Private.

Don't get me wrong. I'm not suggesting we should be running around telling anyone and everyone who'll listen when we last looked at porn, last fantasized about another woman or man, or last rubbed one out in the shower.

Definitely not the fodder I would use for small talk while waiting for my venti coffee in the line at Starbucks.

But when we are in the company of others who claim to be our friends, who act as if they love us, or are part of a common effort to achieve the same noble purpose, clinging to our privacy is counterproductive and does not position us well for ongoing success and personal growth. And when we are actively seeking to improve our lives and strengthen our character, we should not feel shamed for doing so.

I suppose the reason we act this way is because when we open up and expose ourselves to accountability, we give up control and the false notion of safety. But often what makes us so vulnerable to begin with are the secrets we carry around..

The Tight Fisted Fallacy

One of the most ironic aspects of the way we handle our secrets and private matters is that we mistakenly believe the tighter the hold we keep on these things, the safer we are and the less pain we need to face. This is why so many people walk around maintaining an iron-fisted grip around the more intimate details of their lives.

But here is the paradox.

What makes us so vulnerable to pain is the fact that we have something to protect in the first place. Think about it:

> You can break into my house only if I don't invite you in.

You can sell my data only if that data is worth protecting.

You can pick my pocket only if I have something in my pocket to pick.

And you can hurt me by exposing my secrets only if I have secrets to be exposed.

Bill Clinton recognized this when he ran for president. Gary Hart not so much.

Gary Hart was a popular Democratic presidential candidate in 1988. His youth and "new" ideas made him an attractive option to many voters. But rumors of his womanizing started to circulate until a reporter asked him to comment on the matter. He declined.

Unfortunately for him, reporters kept digging around until they exposed an alleged affair he had with a woman named Donna Rice. Gary tried to fight against all the charges and innuendos, but eventually succumbed to the political pressure suspending (and eventually ending) his campaign when the *Washington Post* threatened to run a story about a woman he "had dated" while separated from his wife.

When Bill Clinton first ran for president in 1992, he also faced a potential media-stoked scandal. This time, the focus fell on the alleged use of marijuana rather than a sexual tryst. However, unlike his disgraced predecessor, when asked about this charge, the sharp-witted then-Arkansas governor got out in front of everyone and admitted he had indeed experimented with the illegal substance stating, *"I've never broken a state law … but when I was in England,*

I experimented with marijuana a time or two, and I didn't like it. I didn't inhale it, and never tried."

Understand that while his "admission" was a bit weak, not copping to any actual inhalation, the fact that he, a presidential candidate, was willing to admit any drug experimentation at all was extremely noteworthy. Most certainly, his decision to be at least somewhat transparent about this misstep proved to be a wise move, diffusing any potential scandals that could have perpetuated had he been dishonest or evasive.

Bill Clinton ended up moving past this little incident with ease, eventually winning the presidential elections of 1992 and 1996.

Two different presidential candidates.
Two different "scandals."
Two different outcomes.

Why?

Because while Hart painted a bull's-eye on his back through his secrecy and dishonesty, Clinton cleared the political table, remaining open handed about his choices and leaving any would-be detractors zero ammo with which to take aim and fire at him.

In other words, Clinton gave the media and his political rivals no story to run with, and in doing so, he insulated himself from any further damage.

We could all learn a lesson from Bill Clinton.

Recognize that while much could be said about his decision to smoke marijuana at all, or the fact that his claim of not inhaling seemed feeble at best, he understood that by not hiding what many would see as a flaw or weakness gave him a perceived quality of integrity and made what could have easily been "juicy" tabloid fodder a non-story.

What if we adopted this type of open-handed approach to our own personal struggles and weaknesses when it comes to our churches and relationships? What if instead of protecting our "secret sins," we owned them openly, refusing to indulge the shame that usually accompanies those secrets?

We'd flip the script.

Rather than being a target for gossipers who seek to expose our flaws in their pathetic attempts to maintain social relevance, we'd stand out as examples of authenticity and integrity that others could aspire to be.

The truth is when someone is able to dish dirt on you about personal struggles that you are trying to keep secret, you afford that individual a certain amount of power over you. But when you live with transparency and refuse to hide your flaws, you take the power away and reduce that person to the rumor-mongering asshole they really are.

What so many of us fail to understand is that the safety our privacy and secrecy promises is not really safe at all, but an illusion. By keeping our struggles and insecurities private and in the dark, we give our secrets a place to fester and grow until they get too big for the tight confines we create, leading to our ultimate exposure and disgrace.

The paradoxical truth is this…

Vulnerability leads to invulnerability and inner strength, while secrecy and privacy lead to susceptibility and weakness. And while strength sometimes requires an iron fist, often what will keep us the strongest is an open hand.

Chapter 8

WELL, THAT WAS AWKWARD – A LESSON IN VALUES

My wife and I try to have sex somewhat regularly. Admittedly, during certain seasons of life among the chaos, "regularly" might be more of a moving target, but we don't have a set number of times a month we try to hit or a calendar that keeps track of our "sex nights."

Regardless, "regularly" works well for us.

Why do I bring this up?

Truthfully, because there's a better than average chance you might still be reeling from my earlier suggestion that sharing one's marital sexual frequency could be a healthy topic for a small group discussion. Mind you, not any small group. Only a group where there's real intimacy and deep relationships among the members.

Side note: If you are part of a more typical church small group where conversations are relatively on the surface, and the most intimate part of your life that gets shared is your preferences for certain brands of coffee, then I would not recommend this direction at all. You might not get invited back.

But I digress.

The truth is, I fully appreciate how small group sex talk may make many people extremely uncomfortable. After all, that's very private stuff, right? But that's the point, if you haven't figured it out already.

Discomfort is a good thing.

I know all too well that discussing sexual frequency is going to be a challenging and extremely uncomfortable idea.

I know it will offend a few people.

I know it will draw some criticism.

I know my suggestion will result in a few less great book reviews.

But that's OK.

Because nothing worth anything comes without some discomfort. (My deepest apologies to all the grammar teachers out there.) And what we all need to understand is that most of the time, the only reason we feel certain topics and conversations are awkward is because we make them that way.

Stop for a moment and think about this sex discussion idea critically. Indulge me, and follow along before writing me off as a lunatic.

First, the number of times you have sex with your spouse in a given week or month is just a number. That's it. Yes, I understand it's a "private" number, but it's a simple statistic nonetheless. Once, twice, five times, whatever—*we are just dealing with a numerical figure.*

Second, the common assumption (yes, assumption) is that if you are married, you are having sex (with each other—that's an important detail!) with some sort of frequency. Now I know this is not the case with many couples, but we'll get to that later.

Third, like it or not, sexual frequency is an indicator of marital health. It's by no means the only indicator, and it can even be a misleading one at that. But, generally speaking, couples in happy, thriving marriages have regular sex **that's physically and spiritually fulfilling for both parties.**

Put that all together, and I think it's fair to say that sexual frequency serves as a fairly good gauge or KPI (key performance indicator) for the health of one's marriage.

It's a lot like website analytics.

The amount of traffic or visitors you get says a lot about your website. Now it doesn't say everything about your site, because there is such a thing as "bad" traffic. But, if you are getting little to no traffic, that's probably indicative of an issue that needs to get fixed.

Some sites need a lot of traffic to survive.

Some need less.

It all depends on the website.

But they all need some.

And so, when we are talking about sex and marriage, what makes this stuff so sensitive is the fact that we deem it such. If I'm having sex with my wife regularly (defined by us) and we are happy with the frequency, what's so embarrassing about saying that?

I'm not taking and sharing pictures of us in action.

We aren't talking about our favorite positions and such.

No one is saying how long or short our lovemaking sessions last.

No, we are just stating what should already be assumed. We are happily married, and we like to have "regular" sex whenever possible. Our definition of "regular" may not match up to yours, and for me, that's not embarrassing. If you are having sex more often than us, that's fine. I'm not here to compare or win some sort of sex prize, because what works for us works really well.

It's only awkward if we make it awkward.

Now, do you know what would be awkward? If we weren't having sex at all. Or if the last time we had sex was when Obama got into office. Yeah, that'd be a different story.

But why?

Again, a number is just a number. But it's what that number says about us and our relationship. It's the fact that a big fat goose egg in the "how many times we've had sex in the past year" column would signal to others what we already know to be true—*that our marriage may not be quite as good as what everyone thinks.*

The reasons for that could be many outside of legitimate medical or health-related reasons.

Maybe one or both spouses are addicted to pornography so there's some real pain and trust issues going on. Maybe someone is having a physical or emotional affair. Maybe one spouse grew up with a really disjointed and oppressive sexual theology that still haunts him or her to this day. Maybe it's all of that, or maybe it's none of that. But it's something, and that something is likely impacting the quality of that marriage.

But here's the kicker.

Even that awkwardness is unmerited. Because the shame that comes along with it is like all other instances of shame. It's created in our minds. And the worst-case scenarios we spin up in our heads either won't happen or shouldn't be entertained at all.

Yes, some people might judge your marriage.

Sure, some people may be tempted to gossip about you.

Some people may condescendingly pity you.

But most won't.

And, the ones who do aren't really worth a moment of your time or concern, because your real friends will be more concerned with coming alongside you to walk out the process of healing rather than making judgments about you. And if you value your marriage, then your main concern should be getting it back on track rather than trying to manage your manufactured marital façade.

The choice is simple.

Avoid making things awkward and remain stuck in your discontentment.

Or refuse to buy into the shame and be honest about your reality, so there's room for challenging, growing, and healing.

Falling Forward

I remember getting my friend Mike's accountability report emailed to me. This was a weekly occurrence, as the accountability software he was using would automatically send me, his designated accountability partner, a list of sites he had visited in the past week that were "questionable" (if any).

I called him up with some sense of excitement because it had been four weeks since he had last visited any adult sites, according to his reports. Mike was a younger guy in my church who had approached me about helping him with his long-standing porn use, and so seeing that he had made some real progress was very encouraging.

Mike answered the phone.

"Hey Carl, what's up?"

I replied, "Nothing, man, just wanted to tell you that your accountability report was good again. What's it been—a month since you last checked out a porn site?"

Mike remained silent for a moment, and then he said, "Uh, yeah, about that. I turned off the accountability stuff. I've been looking at porn pretty regularly, but I was just too embarrassed to tell you."

Ugh, balloon popped.

I said, "Oh, man, that sucks. Bro, you know the whole point of having me as your accountability partner is, so I can hold you accountable?"

"Yeah, I know," he quietly responded. "Man, I just felt too stupid to tell you."

At that point I said, "Mike, first know that I love you, and whether or not you mess up doesn't change anything. But, I don't want to waste my time and yours if you're not going to be honest with me—good or bad."

After a short pause, he said, *"OK, I understand. So am I just supposed to screw up again and again and again and just let you see those reports?"*

"EXACTLY!" I replied. *"Mike, you are doing this to get better and improve things. You can't do that if you lie to me. Don't turn off your accountability software if you are going to watch porn. Instead, if you're going to fail, have the integrity to fail out in the open. Better to fall forward than pretend you haven't fallen at all."*

He agreed that he would remain honest with me moving forward and then hung up.

What's the point here?

It shows how a life focused on avoiding embarrassment, shame, and awkwardness is a life that's usually lacking or completely devoid of growth. The topics and discussions we tend to circumnavigate are the very ones that will often challenge us the most.

We don't talk about our sex lives (or lack thereof) because it's uncomfortable and may signal to those around us that there's a deficiency in our marriage.

Mike lied about his internet activity by disabling his accountability software because his repeated failures would possibly communicate to me a shortcoming in his character.

Identify any topic or subject in your life that is a bit of a sore spot that you try to avoid at all costs, and chances are the reason you do so is that you don't want to face the potential consequences of engaging in that problematic behavior or belief.

But it's in those difficult moments and "awkward" conversations where you can often experience the most growth and improvement. Yeah, it sucks when you have to go through that process, but there's tremendous value in doing so, and as the Marines say, you have to "embrace the suck."

Unfortunately, what prevents us from doing so is that we tend to devalue what's valuable, and we place far too much value on what is, for the most part, worthless.

Stuff and Sh*t

Legendary comedian George Carlin was well known for his surly and sarcastic comedy style. In one of his more famous routines, he poked fun at materialism and the difference between how we value our property as opposed to the property of others. A rather notable moment in his act was when Carlin said, *"Have you ever noticed that their stuff is shit, and your shit is stuff?"*

Now, language aside, Carlin's observation when it comes to the value we place on our "stuff" versus other people's "shit" is pretty spot on, and it accurately spotlights the way we tend to overvalue certain things and devalue other things.

And while I have no intention or interest in breaking down the perils of materialism, I do think there is a lesson here that can be applied to how we avoid awkward topics in our lives because of the threat those matters pose to what we value—or our "stuff," if you will.

For instance, we would rather avoid conversations about our sex lives because what we say may reflect poorly on our marriages. We don't want our relationships to look dysfunctional or inferior to the "amazing" relationships we feel other people are busy enjoying. So, rather than lying about our situations or inviting some scrutiny, it's far more preferable to avoid the topic altogether.

This way our "stuff" stays safe.

Our reputations stay intact.
Our images remain unharmed.
Our polished marriages stay bright, shiny, and pristine.

But in the process of doing this, we devalue what's truly important.

So much for marital satisfaction.

So much for intimacy building.

So much for honesty.

We say we value these things, but by focusing on the other "stuff," we end up treating the real "stuff" like crap.

It's the same thing with Mike and his dishonesty.

Mike's real problem wasn't so much his porn use (although that is, of course, a problem). And it wasn't even his dishonesty. It was that he placed tremendous value on the wrong priority.

See, Mike was more concerned with what I thought about him than getting healthier. He subordinated his need for growth and healing to the demands of maintaining a sterling image. Ultimately, his value system was severely messed up, and that resulted in him placing too much importance on the wrong thing and not enough importance on the right thing.

He cared about the wrong "stuff."

And listen, we all do this. We care way too much about what's fleeting, fickle, and out of our control, and in the process, we neglect the weightier matters of life. We place value on the valueless and avoid the awkward to pursue the inconsequential.

The truth is there will always be topics and conversations that push our comfort zones and cause us to feel awkward. But when we reprioritize our values and focus on the "stuff" that really matters, navigating these situations becomes a whole lot easier.

The First Time I Masturbated

I grew up in a family where sex wasn't ever talked about, so everything I "learned" came from my friends, and let's just say they weren't always the best sources of information.

My parent's unwillingness to dive into these areas of interest not only left me with a lot questions regarding sex and the like, but it also signaled to me that they were not a reliable or safe source I could look to when I needed advice. And while it's certainly not their fault that I turned to porn at a young age, their absence in this area of my life definitely didn't help things at all.

Conversely, since I am a person who generally tries to learn from his mistakes, my wife and I have always been very proactive with our kids when it comes to talking about sex, porn, and so on. In fact, the first talk I had with my son Hunter about sex was when he was only six years old. The reason we are so aggressive with these conversations is because we know that the sooner we bridge these topics, the greater the chance is that they will listen to us, and the more likely they will be to view us as safe people they can go to whenever they have questions.

That being said, we certainly aren't perfect. We've both dropped the ball at times. In my case, it was the wet dream and masturbation ball that ended up hitting the floor with my son. Honestly, I don't know why or what I was thinking, but while I had multiple chats with my son about sex and porn over the years, the two topics I failed to address were wet dreams and masturbation.

Crazy…

Was it that I didn't really think that was an important conversation to have?

No, for sure it's important.

Was it that I didn't think boys his age didn't experience these things?

Haha, that's a good one!

Or was it that subconsciously I knew it was an uncomfortable conversation, so it conveniently "slipped my mind" over and over again?

I don't know for sure, but I do know this. When my son turned thirteen, I needed to fix that oversight and do so quickly because time was ticking. I knew all too well what happens when parents don't engage with their kids on these matters, and it never ends up good—mostly because if we fail to educate our children properly on the realities of sex and sexual anatomy, they will inevitably form their own opinions and come up with their own vocabulary to define their experiences. Ultimately, I had to act on what I claimed to value (that being the welfare of my children), and awkwardness be damned.

So looking for a reason to bridge this conversation, I took my son aside one day and asked him if he had ever experienced a wet dream. Or as I put it, *"Hey, Hunter, have you ever woken up with what felt like a sticky mess in your pants?"*

He laughed and then looked at me strangely and said, *"No, why?"*

I kept it nonchalant and just replied, *"No biggie. But you are getting to the age when you will, and when you do, I want you to know two things. First, it's going to seem totally gross. Second, it's totally natural. So when it does happen, let me know, because it happened to me too, and I know how strange it felt for me the first time."*

He agreed, and we both went about our business.

Admittedly, I could have used a better word than "gross," but I was just trying to speak in a manner that a boy his age would appreciate. After all, when I had my first wet dream, I felt weirded out, gross, and embarrassed. But again, this is what happens when we don't start these needed conversations (that's plural) at a younger age. We attach negative or misleading terms and meanings to what in actuality is part of God's genius and beautiful design. Unfortunately, in this case, I was playing catch up, so Hunter didn't get the benefit of having those talks prior.

Call it coincidence, providence, or just plain dumb luck, but my timing couldn't have been better. Because just one week later, Hunter came into our bedroom one morning and woke me up. I asked him what was up, and he said, *"Hey, Dad, remember that talk we had about waking up with a mess in my pants? Well, it happened."*

I kinda chuckled and said, *"Congrats. Gross, right?"*

He laughed, too. *"Yeah, man. Totally gross."*

I put my hand on his shoulder and said, *"Well, first, thanks for telling me. Second, again it's natural, so don't freak out. Third, let's talk later today. I have something else I want to tell you. Cool?"*

He said yeah, and after giving me a Jersey-style fist bump, he walked out of the room.

Later that day, seizing the opportunity afforded me, I pulled Hunter aside.

"Hey, man, I want to talk to you about something else. Have you heard the word 'masturbate' or 'masturbation'?"

He half smiled and said, *"Yeah."*

I then asked, expecting the worst, *"Do you know what that is?"*

"Nope."

Sighhhhh. Maybe I wasn't too late after all!

Now, before I go on, for those of you who are laughing and thinking to yourself, "Sure, Carl—at least that's what he told you," let me explain. My son is pretty transparent and is a terrible liar to boot. He's always been bad at deception, and having a dad who played a lot of poker in the past has not helped his case when he has tried to pull a fast one. So I am fully confident that he was being 100 percent honest with me.

Now, back to the awkwardness...

I looked at him and said, *"Well, remember that wet dream you had? Masturbation is basically what you call it when you play with yourself down there until you orgasm and have that mess, but you're awake."*

He looked weirded out and made a face.

I continued, *"I know, it sounds strange, but trust me, there will come a point when you might think about doing it. Let me tell you how it happened with me."*

Pause.

I'm guessing at this point some of you reading this are feeling as if your heads are about to explode. Why tell him that I masturbated? And why the heck would I share with him how it happened? Isn't it better just to say it's really bad and end it at that? Maybe even add something about how my hand fell off afterwards and I now use a prosthetic, or how I temporarily went blind. That way he'd be crazy to try it himself.

Hang with me.

"I was about your age, Hunter. I was visiting my grandparents and was taking a shower, and while I was showering, I thought I'd experiment and see what would happen if I touched myself long enough."

He started smiling and kinda chuckled.

"I know. Funny. But let's be honest—it feels kinda good when you touch that, right?"

He nodded his head with a smirk communicating a "Well, you got me on that one" sentiment.

"So anyway, I did that and then kept doing that, and then blammo—it was on like Donkey Kong."

At this point, he was openly laughing. I think it was partly because of the humorous way I explained it, but also because I think he was surprised that I, his father, would be so willing to share such an awkward and somewhat embarrassing moment with him.

I continued,

"So the reason I'm telling you this is because you are going to hear about masturbation sooner or later. And since you have a penis, at some point you may wonder what happens if you play with it long enough. So I want to save you some time and just let you in on a few things.

"First, if you masturbate and orgasm, it's going to feel really good. Scratch that—it will be amazing."

He looked taken back.

"But masturbation is a Pandora's Box, meaning if you go there, you may invite in other problematic issues. See, our brains are designed to bond to what gives us pleasure, and masturbation will give you a whole lot of pleasure. But it's 'pleasure' that's meant to be enjoyed with your wife some day so you can bond with her, not alone in your room with your pants around your ankles or in your grandparents' shower like I did."

I could tell by his face that he was not feeling awkward, but he was really trying to think through what I was telling him.

"It's kinda like basketball. You love shooting hoops. And when you come home, if you had a rough day at school like last year, you'll go shoot hoops often, right?"

He nodded in agreement.

"And that's good, man. That's a great outlet. But the reason you do that is shooting hoops gives your brain pleasure, so when faced with discomfort or stress, your brain's go-to solution is 'Let's go shoot some hoops!'

"But let's just say you decide to masturbate. You are going to open up your brain to a whole new kind of pleasure that it's going to like an awful lot. And our brains are kinda selfish, so instead of shooting hoops, at some point your brain may decide to tell you to skip the basketball and go right to masturbation.

"Now let me ask you, which do you think is healthier? Is it better to spend your afternoon shooting hoops sharpening your game, or locked away in your room with your pants down masturbating?"

He looked at me as if I were an idiot for even asking that question and answered, *"Um, basketball is healthier."*

I answered back,

"Exactly! And what can happen is if you do that long enough, eventually your brain will see masturbation and porn as the way to cope with all sorts of problems in life. And that's really unhealthy. And it can even lead to addiction like it did for me.

"Dude, I spend all my week helping guys who got into their porn use because they decided to try masturbation and porn at a young age. Not because they are terrible people or bad humans, but because they were curious like you might be, or like I was. But then that curiosity led to a habit, and that habit led to a lifelong addiction. That's no way to live."

He started nodding his head in agreement. I could tell some of what I was saying was actually sinking in.

I went on:

"So listen, if you do end up masturbating, please know it's pretty common and doesn't make you some sort of weirdo. But promise me that you'll talk to me about it. I promise you I won't be upset and I won't make it weird. After all, I did it, and it doesn't get much weirder than doing it in your grandparents' shower."

He laughed again and agreed.

"But just know what you are opening yourself up to, and I hope you decide to not do it because of the risks you take on by doing so. Either way, I'll be here for you to talk though the whole thing. Cool?"

He nodded in agreement, gave me a fist bump ('cause that's how we roll), and left the room.

Why do I share this?

First, understand that when you lead difficult conversations with transparency, it allows for a deeper connection. It signals to the other person that you care, empathize, and are a safe place to come to when he or she needs to talk. This is important whether we are talking about a friend, coworker, small group member, spouse, or especially your child.

I can't guarantee it. But I can tell you with a great deal of confidence that if Hunter has questions about sex, masturbation, or porn, there's a good chance he will come to me to talk about it.

Because I get it.

Because I'm safe.

Because it won't be awkward for me.

And that's huge!

Second, this is what happens when you place a value on the right priorities. You can operate with a greater degree of confidence, and with less insecurity and awkwardness, because the stuff that shouldn't really matter, such as opinions and social approval, won't get in the way.

I knew my son's welfare mattered more than my awkwardness.

I knew preparing my son for the inevitable was needed far more than maintaining a high comfort level. And because I dove into this topic with him without awkwardness or shame, it not only turned out well, but it also brought us even closer as a father and son.

Third, we need to be having these talks much earlier and far more frequently, because when we do, we can reduce the likelihood of our children forming negative or misleading conclusions about their sexual experiences. Beyond that, we also need to be aware that there is a strong possibility we might be carrying around some of our own toxic sexual vocabulary and flawed perspectives, and we need to check that mess at the door so we don't pass it along to our kids.

The reality is that there will always be awkward times in life. There will always be those conversations that really push your comfort zone and may seem too tempting to avoid. And if you value the wrong "stuff," your fate is pretty much sealed. But if you place your value on what's truly important such as love, health, growth, and connection, you will find it far easier to navigate these difficult moments. You might just have to push through some initial discomfort.

Chapter 9

THAT CUTS DEEP

The vast majority of my formative education (elementary, middle, and high school) was experienced in a Christian school setting. I'd be lying if I said I enjoyed it. Maybe I'm jaded, but growing up in a Christian school didn't prepare me well for the real world, and it exposed me to a weird Christian subculture that I couldn't wait to detach myself from as soon as I hit college. The few meaningful friendships I formed throughout those years quickly dissolved after graduation.

Of course, a lot of that falls on me. My lack of confidence, my need for fitting in with somebody, and my attitude didn't help my cause. But regardless, feeling like a square peg in a small room of round holes was an unpleasant experience. One of the biggest drawbacks of my school experience was the size of the student body. Classes were super small, so instead of having a variety of "tribes" to pick from as my identified people group, there was only a handful.

The "cool" kids (again, a debatable term).
The not-so-popular kids.
The brainy kids.
The dorks and rejects.

So fitting in became even more important, because there were only so many openings in the groups that actually "mattered."

While I was short and skinny with a big head (picture a baby bird in Dockers and a button-down shirt) and not particularly athletic, I was still interested in females and dating like most boys my age. Not just because of hormones, but also because having a girlfriend helped one's social status. Unfortunately for me, I was already working with a deficit, and in that Christian school, the dating pool was small. Generally, each grade had a handful of "hot" girls that all the boys competed for, creating a really lopsided ratio and poor prospects for baby bird-headed kids like me.

In seventh or eighth grade, I remember we had a couple of new girls join our grade. I recognize that doesn't sound like a big deal to the average public school kid, but in a small Christian school, being the new girl was akin to being a "fish" in a prison. All the inmates wanted a shot. And I was one of those inmates. In addition, these girls were coming from a public school setting, so that was also a HUGE bonus.

One day at lunch, a couple of the guys and I were going around busting balls with each other about who in our group actually had a shot at one of the new girls. That's when a "friend" of mine named Jose looked at me and said, *"Dang, man, you're ugly."* He laughed, and I shot back at him with a quick response, but then he followed up with, *"No, seriously, you're an ugly dude."*

Now, kids say mean stuff to each other all the time. No surprise there. And guys, we are probably the worst when it comes to insulting each other—even friends. But the way Jose said what he said was different. It didn't come off like a jab but an observation. On top of that, Jose wasn't a jerk typically. I actually preferred him over most of my schoolmates. So his comment stung, and the witness to that fact is that over thirty-five years later, I still remember that day, that comment, that pain, and the shame it caused.

Crazy, but true.

And I would venture to say that you probably have had similar situations happen in your life. Maybe it was a parent, teacher, pastor, or some nitwitted schoolmate, but I would bet that there are at least a few times in your life when someone said something to you that was really painful, and you remember that moment just as clearly as the day it happened.

And why?

Because language matters.

Words matter. The pain those verbal attacks cause you matters. And the way we talk about ourselves, our struggles, our shortcomings, and our failures matters because the language we choose can create more shame and pain than you'd ever think possible.

But if you wish to start living your life in spite of shameful feelings, if you want to make decisions based on your values and not opinions, then you need to learn how to talk through life's challenging subjects in a way that creates hope and encouragement rather than condemnation and self-loathing.

And while our words can truly cut deeply like a knife, they also have the ability to open up opportunities for growth when we don't fear them.

The D Word

Have you ever had one of those days when everything seems relatively smooth and stable and then BAM! here comes a monkey wrench that quickly gets thrown into your plans? Hello, unwelcome interruption! About five years ago, my wife came home from work and said, *"Hey, Carl, I think you need to have a talk with your son tonight."*

I thought to myself, what did Hunter do now? And so, fearing the worst, I replied, *"OK, what's up?"*

"Well, his teacher called me today," she went on. *"Apparently, he said the word 'dick' to a couple of kids."*

Admittedly, I chuckled under my breath and then assured her I would have a chat with him. She said thanks and assured me that it was probably something innocent, so give him some slack. I agreed.

A little later I had to run an errand, so I asked my son to come along as my copilot. He eagerly agreed, jumped into the front seat of my Jeep, and buckled his seat belt, and we took off. After a few minutes of catching up on his day, I decided it was time to have our chat.

"Hey, buddy, Mommy said your teacher called her and said you used a word today that's not really appropriate."

He looked surprised and asked, *"What word?"*

"Dick."

What he said next surprised me: *"Yep."* Then he went on, *"You know, Dad, like Moby Dick."*

Two words: <u>instant relief</u>. I thought to myself, "Well, this just got a whole lot easier."

But then he said, *"Why is that a problem?"*

Oh boy. Here we go.

See, while admittedly part of me would have rather avoided that talk all together (at his age), my wife and I had committed to the idea of being as open and honest as possible concerning sensitive topics with our kids, even if we feared by doing that we might open up a small Pandora's box of issues. I know it sounds like a risky parenting strategy, but for context, let me backtrack to a few years earlier.

[Cue time machine noise]

When my son was younger, he really loved sharks. Actually, he loved all dangerous animals, but sharks? Yeah, they were the badasses of the sea. So when I saw a video on Twitter that had gone viral of a man in Australia who jumped off a cliff into the harbor, only to land about twenty feet away from a great white shark, I thought, *"Man, Hunter would love this!"*

What was so awesome about the video footage was that it was taken from a GoPro camera strapped on the man's helmet, so you could watch the whole thing unfold from a first-person point of view.

And while the man in the video lived, at the end of the video, after swimming to shore, he took off his helmet, looked into the camera, and rightfully said, "Holy shit!" Honestly, I can't think of a more fitting thing to say in a situation as crazy as that one.

Regardless, both my son (age six) and daughter (age nine) were fairly young at the time, so I had some reservations about letting them see the video. Maybe I could turn off the clip before the "holy shit" moment to prevent them from hearing that word, rightfully fearing that Hunter would just run around the house for the rest of the day repeating it.

But then I thought about it and I said to myself, *"What am I doing here? They are going to hear this word sooner or later, so I might as well explain to them what it means and why (at their age) it's not something they should be saying."*

So we sat down to watch the video, and before I started it, I told them that at the end of the video the man being filmed used the word "shit," which means "poop." They both started laughing uncontrollably (especially my son), and for a brief moment I thought to myself, *"What a dumb idea, Carl."*

But at that point, I had already crossed the line, so I just pushed ahead and hit "play."

After we had watched the whole clip and my kids slowed down with their laughter, I asked them if they had ever heard the word "shit" before. My son shook his head and emphatically said "no," but my daughter sheepishly nodded her head and said that she had. When I asked her where, she said, *"A boy on the bus who is 'bad' and doesn't believe in God said it."*

PAUSE.

Do you see what happened there?

I almost didn't talk to my kids about a "curse word" because I wanted to shelter them and avoid all the messiness of introducing a new vocabulary term to their knowledge base. But, as it turned out, my daughter had already heard the word. Worse yet, she had formed the completely misguided opinion that people who said that word were "bad" and atheists!

As parents and individuals, we love our little comfort zones. We worry that engaging in these uncomfortable conversations may inadvertently lead to even worse problems. But often the potential catastrophes we seek to avoid are less real than the immediate negative consequences we experience when we indulge our fears and anxieties.

And so with Hunter, for me the clear choice was to answer his questions about why the word "dick" wasn't appropriate, and that's exactly what I did. Not only that, but I also went through ALL the "bad" words that refer to body parts, explaining why they were inappropriate, hurtful, and/or demeaning along the way (occasionally reminding him that if he ever said certain words, his mother would certainly kill him).

Again, words matter. And how we choose to approach these conversations assigning values, meanings, and associations to certain terms along the way matters. Whether it's talking about porn and masturbation in your small group, or "potty language" and body part slang words with your kids, we need to be ever mindful that these occasions provide teachable growth moments that benefit both parties and should be pursued rather than avoided.

The choice to be more proactive about matters of language (both sexually and nonsexually related) has proved to be fruitful when it comes to our children. For one, we know that when they hear something on TV or at school, there's no need to freak out, because our kids understand what's OK, what's not, and why. They have a greater appreciation for the reasons that certain terms should be avoided or should be used only in a certain context beyond just "that's bad" or "that's good."

It also keeps conversations in our house far more open and inviting, because both my son and daughter recognize that they have a safe place to talk about difficult things or to ask sensitive questions without sending Mom and Dad into a state of panic. This sense of "safety" leads to a greater feeling of trust from our children, because they know that should they step too far over the line, rather than a swift kick to the butt, they will receive a measure of grace along with a thoughtful explanation.

Don't get me wrong—our kids know we have standards. They understand that if we've covered a certain area of interest and determined that it's inappropriate for them to keep discussing it, there will be consequences should they decide to "go there." But again, they know the why behind the what, and so what they choose to say and don't say is more about the reason than the rules.

Penis, Vagina, and Other "Naughty" Words

Kids are silly, but they are an easy audience to please if you're an aspiring entertainer. Literally anything can capture their attention if there's an adequate amount of cuteness, nonsense, or energy involved. Just take a look at what your kid watches on TV, and you'll gain a clear appreciation for their very rudimentary sense of quality.

Tell your child a joke laced with clever sarcasm and wit, expect a blank stare back accompanied with a high degree of boredom. But share with them the latest stock market trends, interjecting a plethora of fart and burp noises along the way, and you'll have someone who is mesmerized with your display of comic genius.

Seriously, the stuff that makes a child laugh uncontrollably is flat-out nonsense. But it's expected. Because kids lack both maturity and life experience, when you make noises that are in actuality very natural, or say words that just sound super strange (like vagina), you will very likely be met with a deluge of laughter and chuckles. Then we grow up.

Or do we?

The truth is that despite our age or station in life, certain terms still feel weird or uncomfortable to say, especially words related to sex and sexuality, because they trigger some sort of uneasiness within us due the cultural hedges we've placed around them. I've been working in this area of ministry for over a decade, and if I'm being perfectly honest, it still feels very different when I say a word such as "penis" or "masturbation" than when I say "elbow" or "firehouse."

I know, it sounds strange that particular words would trigger certain feelings in our body, but this phenomenon has been evidenced in such linguistic studies as the one conducted by the Department of Experimental Psychology at the University of Bristol.

In this experiment, participants read aloud "swear" words and euphemisms of the swear words (i.e., the "F-word"), while electrodermal activity was monitored by a device that measured changes in skin resistance in response to an applied DC voltage source.

The key finding from this study was that autonomic responses to swear words were larger than to other euphemisms and neutral words, leading researchers to conclude that the heightened response to swear words reflected a form of verbal conditioning in which the phonological form of the word was directly associated with an affective response.[18]

Or if you want to skip the clinical terminology, when individuals read certain words considered culturally taboo, they experienced a tangible negative emotional response that could be detected in their skin's electrodermal activity.

Why is this significant?

Because as researchers note, it is typical behavior for people to avoid talking about taboo matters due to the risk they run of having to say taboo words.[19] And let's be real, even though in recent years we've seen some changes here, the truth remains that sexual terms generally are viewed as taboo by the predominant culture outside of highly specific scenarios. Therefore, it shouldn't be surprising that we see a general avoidance of discussing sexually related matters outside of designated "safe zones" such as a support group.

This begs the question, why are these words so taboo in the first place?

Why is there such an aversion to language related our sex and sexuality? After all, sex is a fundamental part of existence and is needed for procreation and the survival of our species. It's a good gift from God and is meant to be enjoyed and explored with our spouses to increase intimacy and connection. It is in every way a critical part of our core identity. Additionally, our bodies are marvelous creations of God with all its parts serving a specific function with a unique purpose. As the apostle Paul notes, "Our bodies have many parts, and God has put each part just where he wants it."

Yet we refrain from using such words as penis, vagina, masturbation, and the like in everyday conversation because of the cultural discomfort they create. We've in essence built a wall around certain terms and conversations because that wall protects the status quo.

Don't misunderstand—I'm not saying that we need to force certain words into conversations where they don't belong. There's no legitimate reason to start talking about your penis or vagina with your accountant when reviewing your tax situation. But simply avoiding these words because of the awkwardness they create leads to a sexually repressive environment where those who need help, have questions, or just want to learn will feel discouraged to initiate these types of discussions.

Sexual words are not "naughty" or "bad." They are just that—*sexual*. And that's OK. So we need to focus more on the context in which these terms are used rather than the terms themselves. Sure, "penis" is not a typical word you'd hear at the average family dinner table. But there's no reason it shouldn't be if your child has questions because of something a schoolmate said to him that day. Likewise, masturbation is likely not going to come up in your coffee bar chats at church, but if it does, then fine, because engaging in those conversations may help someone get the help and answers he or she needs.

Language matters. And the hedges we place around our vocabulary matter too because of the message those hedges send to the people around us.

Labels Are for T-shirts

Perhaps one of the most important aspects of our language is the words we use to describe ourselves and our choices, particularly when it comes to the struggle of shame. While avoiding uncomfortable conversations or not seeking help simply because of a resistance to taboo matters certainly hurts us, the words we choose to label ourselves and the decisions we make can be even more damaging. But just like curse words or "naughty" sex words, what makes these descriptive terms so impactful isn't the words themselves, but what we associate with those words.

For instance, take the word "addict."

Merriam-Webster defines addict as *"one exhibiting a compulsive, chronic, physiological or psychological need for a habit-forming substance, behavior, or activity."* It's a legitimate clinical term used to describe a chemical or behavioral dependency. There is no moral component to this definition. It's simply a word used to categorize a factual observation. Yet, when we hear the word "addict" or "addiction," we immediately connect it to all sorts of negative thoughts and stereotypes.

No one wants to be called an addict.

No one wants to say, "I'm married to an addict."

But yet some people are addicts. Some people are married to addicts. And while that's unfortunate and not a reason for celebration, it's a fact of life, and recognizing the truth of your situation should only motivate you to seek help and healing, not find a hole to jump into so you can bury yourself with excessive shame.

This is why when asked if chronic porn use is an "addiction," I tell people that I don't care much for labels. Define it however you want. The only question you should ask yourself is if you have a behavior that you can't seem to put down and if that behavior is blowing up your life. If the answer is yes, then you need to get some help and stop trying to categorize your level of dependency to avoid the stigmas you've bought into.

Or worse yet, don't label yourself as an addict to confirm the negative feelings you have about who you are as a person. This, unfortunately, happens as well. Due to past pain, abandonment, and emotional neglect, we form unhealthy opinions about ourselves, and rather than going through the internal conflict we would create by critically examining our opinions, it's easier to say and do things that just reaffirm the lies we've grown up on.

I've been told all my life I'm no good.

I have never felt worthy of love.

I seek acceptance but always fall short.

No one has ever acted like I matter.

And I guess I don't—because I'm an "addict." And while it hurts to come to grips with my inferiority, at least I can have some peace knowing that I deserve the way people have treated me over the years. After all, I'm an addict.

But being "an addict" doesn't define your character or worth. It doesn't mean you are *less than* or beyond hope. It just means you need help. Labels may categorize you, but they never should define you. Because while the word "addict" may accurately describe your ailment, it doesn't describe the entirety of who you are.

You are more than a label.

Words as Weapons

Sticks and stones may break my bones, but names will never hurt me.

I'm sure you are very familiar with that childhood saying. It's been repeated literally millions of times across all the playgrounds and schoolyards of the world. It's a great sentiment, to be honest, but it's just not terribly accurate.

If one was to tweak that saying to better match the realities of life, it would read more like this:

> Sticks and stones may break my bones, which quite frankly sucks and will be a bit painful in the short term. But words will hurt me far worse and the pain will last far longer than you could ever imagine. Sure, maybe right now it's not so bad, but years later when I'm talking to a therapist, I will realize the anguish you caused me and that I've been carrying around that baggage for years but just suppressing it (starting today). So if it wouldn't be too much trouble, I'll go for the sticks and stones if that option is still on the table.

Of course, this isn't how things work. We don't get that option.

Words get thrown around all the time with little regard or concern for the damage they cause. The sticks and stones of our past get buried in the dirt while the pain words cause gets buried in our hearts and minds. Admittedly there will be times when words don't hurt because there is no emotional connection to the person saying them. But then there will be those occasions when words might as well be razor-sharp arrows because the person talking is someone we care about or we look to as an authority.

This is especially unfortunate when the damage inflicted is unintentional or even well meaning.

For example, some time back, I stumbled across a post on Instagram linking to an article written by a Christian author from another Christian "anti-porn" organization addressing the issue of masturbation. The title of the post was *"Is Masturbation Wrong??"*

Realize that when it comes to masturbation, I have seen so many opinions and teaching on this subject. And to be frank, so much of it is complete crap. Very little of what I have read actually encourages healthy conversation and engagement. It falls on the side of either affirmation or shameful rhetoric and focuses only on the actual behavior while generally ignoring the context for the behavior.

And I believe that when it comes to the issue of masturbation, context is everything.

Let's be real, the Bible doesn't have much to say about masturbation. There is no "Thou shalt not masturbate" verse that I can find. Nor does the Bible talk about the negative impact masturbation can have on a person's brain and its highly addictive nature.

However, while the Bible is very quiet when it comes to the morality of rubbing one out, it's chock full of teaching regarding how we should treat people and not use them for our own selfish purposes. And at the end of the day, the primary issue with masturbation is that it is often being done in the context of objectifying someone. In other words, it takes a complete human being (mind, body, and soul) and reduces him down to a physical object for the purposes of sexual gratification. And that's decidedly opposed to the teachings of Jesus.

Yet, 99 percent of the time when Christians talk about masturbation, they fixate solely on finding a hard YES or NO resolution to the question of its permissibility.

All that said, I allowed my curiosity to get the better of me and clicked the article link. Hoping for a fresh take on a touchy subject (no pun intended), I dove in and started reading, but it took only a few minutes before I regretted that decision.

Here are just a few quotes from that article:

> *One of the fundamental issues with masturbation is that our only role in the sex act is that of* **porn director***.*

> *During masturbation we're taking people who haven't given themselves to us and we're compelling them to pleasure us according to our demands. If this happened outside of our minds it would be called **rape**. Of course, this is only happening in our minds. But why should that rinse off the **filth** from the action?*
>
> *The gospel gives us a choice of being **porn directors** and **abusers**, or of being "a chosen people." Let's put away our harem and put on hope. Let's cease to be **predators** so that we can become priests.*

YIKES!

My biggest issue with this piece was not necessarily the conclusions or teaching points of the author (although they were pretty off base, in my opinion), but rather the language and the direction he chose to go in communicating the severity of what he saw as a very problematic behavior.

He used such words as predator, mental rape, porn director, and abuser.

Really shocking and extreme language. If you were reading his piece and struggled with masturbation, your natural reaction would be to find a corner of the room and crawl into the fetal position, opting to completely shut down rather than reaching out to someone for help. And who would blame you? What person in his right mind wants to self-identify as a rapist, abuser, or predator?

Of course, there is something to be said for boldness and speaking from conviction. Calling out "sin" as sin, while being a favorite pastime for many Christians, does have a place in modern culture. But, when you use such words as evil, perverted, twisted, predator, and abuser, you also communicate a high level of condemnation and shame. This applies whether you hear someone else saying it or if you are the one using these descriptions to classify your own behavior.

However, when you choose to use words such as healthy versus unhealthy, or broken and hurt versus whole and complete, you communicate the seriousness of one's poor choices without attaching a high degree of shame. Understand, we are all "sinful" beings who need Jesus, but recognizing that fact does not require us to label our adverse behaviors in a way that reinforces just how disgusting and evil we are.

When you talk about porn and masturbation as twisted or perverted, it reduces the hope of reconciliation, because those words impart a sense of depravity that's beyond reason and sensibility. But when you intentionally use such words as broken, hurt, or unhealthy, you also communicate that there is an opportunity for "fixing," for healing, and for recovery. And don't we all want an opportunity for redemption?

Ultimately, the language and words we use or avoid altogether say a lot about what we fear or believe. Words in the end are just words. But social constructs and cultural influence apply meaning to those words that go far beyond the original intent of their definition.

There is no harm or shame in talking about what God created to be good and enjoyable. Whether you are the one who's hurting, the one who's been hurt, or just a disinterested third party, know that a big step in reducing the shame people feel regarding matters of sex, sexuality, and sexual brokenness lies in redeeming the language we use and talking about these topics in a way that elicits hope and grace rather than condemnation and shame.

Chapter 10

GUT CHECK TIME

I magine this…

You're on a wooden boat in the middle of a chaotic storm on a sea that's known for its temperamental nature. Additionally, you've grown up in a culture that views the sea as a powerful source of chaos that brings with it a great risk of danger to those foolish or brave enough to take it on. You come from a people who aren't exactly a seafaring bunch. To make things worse, it's nighttime, and the guy who's your leader and is kind of responsible for dragging your butt out that night isn't even on the dang boat.

Do you have that picture in your head? Not exactly an ideal situation, and it most certainly is a perilous one.

Now, here's where it gets really crazy!

You hear a voice and you look out on the waters. In the distance through the pouring rain and crashing waves, you see your leader (you know, the guy who's the reason you are out in that storm to begin with), and he is walking on the water. You think, *"What? Are you serious?"*

You rub your eyes to make sure you aren't seeing things. You squint, blink a few times, and what do you know, he's still there. You are taken back because you've never seen anyone do something like that, but this guy does crazy stuff all the time, so you are also not completely shocked. Then he does the most insane thing. He calls out to you and says to climb out of the boat and walk toward him.

That's right, this mysterious leader and teacher you've been pledging allegiance to just called you out. He wants you to step out of your sorta safe boat onto water in the middle of a raging storm and walk toward him. Can you say insane request?

This was the situation Peter faced.

Now for those who don't come from a faith background, you might be wondering who Peter is and what story book I'm pulling this from. Just be patient.

But for those of you who do come from a Christian faith background, you are very familiar with this account and already know the ending. Peter, one of Jesus' twelve disciples, gets out on the water, takes a couple steps toward Jesus (the guy calling him), but then is overcome with fear and doubt and starts to sink, crying out to his teacher for help in the process.

If the disciples had Twitter back then, you know there would have been a dozen or so GIFs and memes floating around later that day showing Peter sinking with the hashtag #FailMoment.

That being said, I think Peter often gets a bad rap. Yes, his faith faltered and yes, he needed his rabbi to bail him out. But he was the only one of his group who had the guts to get out of the boat, putting himself into a situation that in all normal circumstances would have spelled certain death.

This was Peter, though.

A man of action.
A man of conviction.
A man with real moxie.

Peter certainly had his classic fail moments. But with the exception of his denial of Jesus, Peter for the most part was a guy who said what he did and did what he said and didn't offer many apologies in the process. I think Peter may have been from New Jersey, to be honest, but maybe that's just me. If not, he certainly would fit in with our kind.

Regardless, the reason I bring this story up is that "Jersey Pete" faced what I like to call a gut check moment.

Peter had verbally expressed implicit trust in his rabbi.
Peter had followed his rabbi around faithfully.
Peter was for all intents and purposes a true believer.

But now he was faced with a real dilemma. Stay in the boat, which felt a whole lot safer and sensible, or act on what he claimed to believe and value, ignoring the danger of the moment and the feelings of extreme fear and insecurity he was undoubtedly experiencing.

And this is similar to the situations we often face when it comes to confronting our shame.

We know hiding seems safer.

We know avoidance makes sense.

We know staying silent sounds more comfortable.

Ultimately, we know that whatever it is that's creating a shameful moment for us feels overwhelming and as scary as hell. So our instincts are to do what we always do: maintain avoidance and secrecy.

But if our values are in check, we should also recognize that the shame we experience is a lie that needs to be denied along with the power it holds on us. And rather than indulging its ludicrous demands, sometimes we need be a Peter and follow through on what we know and not just what we feel.

A Feeling, Not a Fact

Shame, like any feeling, is hard to recognize for what it truly is. When we are in the grasp of its influence, we lose sight of the reality that what we are experiencing is simply a feeling. In other words, *it's not reality.*

It's a twisted perception of our reality.

Yet so many people allow their feelings to govern the majority of their decisions, giving those feelings far too much authority and allowing them to shape what they believe about their world and themselves, regardless of the facts, often leading to adverse outcomes.

As Herbert Simon, American Nobel Laureate scientist, said in his book Reason in Human Affairs: *"In order to have anything like a complete theory of human rationality, we have to understand what role emotion plays in it. ...* ***Emotion does not always direct our attention to goals we regard as desirable.****"*[20]

Understand that feelings are not a bad thing. Without them, we would just be robotic organisms navigating life as a series of binary choices. There would be no empathy or mercy. No love or kindness. Just black and white, yes or no decisions based solely on a list of metrics. Imagine a world run by Siri or Alexa, except without all the voice recognition errors.

Feelings are what make us human.

They are also a primary reason humanity has survived all these years through hungry dinosaurs, plagues, famines, and the unpredictable whims of mother nature. But feelings are simply meant to serve as a radar system, allowing us to detect *possible* danger or pleasure scenarios so we can formulate appropriate responses.

Scientifically speaking, feelings are the conscious experience of our emotional reactions. They are not factual or certain. Feelings need to be evaluated before being acted upon. Consequently, when we experience shame and fail to recognize that what we are feeling is an unhealthy distortion of reality, we buy into the lies of low self-worth and self-condemnation, turning our back on the promise that what God created is actually "good," falling farther and farther down a toxic rabbit hole.

Of course, this is all easier said than done. Again, feelings are part of our natural makeup and are critical to the most primitive parts of the brain, so simply ignoring them is not an option. We can't just override our biology, nor should we want to. But we also don't need to ride blindly into shame's deep dark spiral.

Two Brains. One Mind.

A few years ago, I was experiencing severe anxiety. I had previous run-ins with the big "A" word, but not quite that bad. The panic attacks, lightheadedness, and chest pain all started kicking in about thirty days into taking on a new role at a company that recruited me for the position of COO. To be honest, I felt unqualified and unsure of myself. This was a brand new responsibility for me, and I didn't know it at the time, but according to my counselor (who I eventually started seeing when sleepless nights and Xanax didn't do the trick any longer), I was experiencing "impostor syndrome."

Wikipedia describes impostor syndrome as follows:

> *Impostor syndrome is a psychological pattern in which an individual doubts their skills, talents, or accomplishments and has a persistent internalized fear of being exposed as a "fraud." <u>Despite</u> external evidence of their competence, those experiencing this*

> *phenomenon remain convinced that they are frauds and do not deserve all they have achieved.*

Did you see that?

> <u>Despite</u> *external evidence of their competence, those experiencing this phenomenon remain convinced that they are frauds and do not deserve all they have achieved.*

Sounds a lot like what we face when dealing with the forces of shame. **Despite** the evidence, **despite** the declarations of God, **despite** everything—we remain convinced that we are "less than" and not worthy of the connection or love we deserve.

Illogical. Unreasonable. Irrational. Senseless. Screwy. Nutty. Wacky.

Despite.

That was me. No matter what my personal history said otherwise, I was convinced that I was not qualified or worthy of the new position I now held. And why? Because the wrong part of my brain was running operations.

See, while all of us have one mind (and sometimes that's debatable when dealing with rush-hour traffic), we have multiple brains. We have a lower brain, midbrain, and upper brain.

The lower brain is your body's emotion center and is where the limbic system resides. Primitive and instinctual, this part of your brain is responsible for behavioral and emotional processes related to survival such as feeding, reproduction, and fight-or-flight responses. In a company scenario, it would be the location manager who handles the day-to-day decision-making choices on the fly to keep operations running smoothly with as few interruptions as possible.

The upper brain, in contrast, is more concerned with logic, reason, and facts. It handles your critical decision-making and has its eye on the big picture. Unlike the lower brain, your upper brain is not ruled by feelings and emotions but by reason. Think of it as your mind's CEO who's consistently trying to guide the manager toward the best long-term decisions for the overall health of the company.

Both of these parts of the brain are involved in your choices. However, your lower brain has more of a "boots on the ground" role and therefore has the upper hand, being the one that ultimately decides any outcome. And here's the bummer: the lower brain will choose to do what causes it the least discomfort and feels best in the moment.

It's kinda selfish that way.

In an ideal situation, while your lower brain is managing your daily life, it would be checking in with your upper brain to make sure that each decision it makes is building toward a better overall future. In my case, while my lower brain was saying, *"Hey, I'm not sure I got this—it's time to panic,"* my upper brain would have been saying, *"Sure you do. Look at the facts. There's no need for worry or fear here.*

Just do what you need to do and stop freaking out 'cause it ain't helping and it's costing you a lot of sleepless nights."

But life is not ideal.

In the end, the reasoning voice of my upper brain was drowned out by the insane rantings of my lower brain. Because of the pain and rejection of my past, I had allowed my manager to run roughshod over all my mental operations, locking away my CEO in some dark boardroom out of sight and out of mind.

And why?

Because as Ryan North, an expert in childhood trauma care, so succinctly states: *"Our brains are wired for connection, but trauma rewires them for protection."*

In other words, without the baggage of abuse, abandonment, and neglect, your lower and upper brains are designed to operate in concert. One makes observations and forms feelings, and the other evaluates the merit of those observations and directs you toward the best decision. But when you experience trauma, your primitive mind takes over, forsaking any concern for what's truly best and opting for what will help you simply survive.

The trick, then, is inviting your upper brain back into the decision-making tango, allowing it to once again operate as the logical and steady voice of reason your lower brain can look to before pulling the trigger on the choices you make.

Admittedly, this requires a level of awareness on your part. It means you need to recognize when facing any decision that you have options, and those options have consequences. And when your upper brain is allowed to speak into those options, hopefully it will convince your lower brain that the ideal path is not only the one that is best, but it is also the one that will feel the best in the end because it most aligns with the values you claim to hold.

Unfortunately, awareness needs to be cultivated. But, if you can develop this habit and allow the space for your two brains to successfully negotiate ideal solutions together, you can work through feelings of shame and moments of discomfort in life, effectively opting for a better path than isolation, self-pity, and secrecy. You can finally work from a place of confidence and worth, rather than indulging the lies that shame whispers in your ears.

The Jig Is Up

Over the past ten years, I have shared my story and past struggle with porn more times than I can count. One-on-one, podcasts, newspaper interviews, and on video—you name it, chances are I did it.

Yep. I'm clearly THE GUY who represents what it looks like to live without shame!

Or so I thought...

About two years ago, I took my daughter to a Phillies baseball game. She was fourteen at the time and was well acquainted with the type of work I did. But, sad to say, I never shared anything about my past or struggle with her or my son. I just kinda kept that little nugget under my hat, figuring there was nothing to be gained by talking about it.

Anyway, there we were, just the two of us, hanging out on a warm summer's night at the ballpark. Things couldn't get better. As we sat there enjoying the game, I received a text from an old friend.

I grabbed my phone and read his message. This guy was someone from my old church who had struggled with porn in the past. He semi-regularly attended the support group I had once hosted at my home for a couple of years.

It had been a while since we last chatted, but I guess he was having a hard time, so he asked me if I could suggest an app to help him block "the bad stuff" on his phone so he could get back on track.

Although I probably should have waited to respond, I texted him back and explained that installing a filter or blocker on his phone would not just make his problem magically go away. I suggested a few resources and action steps (including signing up for the Live Free Community) and told him to follow up with me so we could chat more.

He agreed, and that was it. Oh, and if you were curious, I never heard from him after that. Must have been something I said.

Regardless, I hadn't realized it, but my daughter's teenage curiosity had gotten the better of her, so she had been peeking over my shoulder the whole time I was texting with this guy. It was at that moment when she asked me who I was texting and what we were going back and forth about.

I replied, *"You know what Daddy does, right?"* and then shot her a smirk and sideways glance.

Recognizing that the name of the guy I was chatting with was from our old church, my daughter innocently asked, *"But he's a Christian ... Christians struggle with that stuff, too?"*

I smiled and answered, *"Of course—in fact, just as much as anyone else."*

Thinking I was in the clear, I turned my attention back to the game, grabbed my drink, and sat back in my chair.

That's when my daughter hit me with, *"Have you ever looked at that stuff, Dad?"*

Gulp. Oh man, did she really just ask me that? And at a Phillies game when we are having a good time hanging out? The timing couldn't have been worse.

It was at that moment that I thought to myself, *"Oh man, s*** just got real."*

And no, I don't mean SHAME, although yes, that got real, too.

This was a real crossroads moment. My stomach turned a bit. My pulse rate increased. I thought to myself, *"Why can't someone hit a homerun right now and get me outta this situation?*" But no—of course not. It was the Phillies, who hadn't made the playoffs in over a decade. They clearly weren't going to be of any help.

So I had to act and act fast.

Did I lie and avoid the painful embarrassment of admitting to my daughter that I had struggled with porn nearly all of my life? After all, she seemed so put off by the idea that a Christian man like my friend could be looking at that stuff. Wouldn't this just hurt the image my daughter had of me? It would be so much easier just to tell this little white lie and get back to having a good time with her.

But if I lied, what did that say about me and what I claimed to believe? Did I really drink the same juice I had been peddling the last several years—that shame was an enemy we all needed to deny and not buy into? Maybe I just needed to press on and show the integrity I claimed to value.

But we're talking about my daughter? This would rock her. I just knew it.

My options were simple, and I had only another second or two to act before it started getting really weird for the both of us…

Did I save face and quietly recline in my own shame and hypocrisy, avoiding the disappointment of my own daughter?

Or,

Did I own my crap and practice what I preached?

The shame was undeniable. I could feel it pressing in on all sides. But I also knew the truth. I knew who I really was and the right choice was the only choice. The jig was up, and it was time to face the music, good or bad.

Shame wasn't going to win out this time.

I sat there for another second and finally said, *"Yeah, I struggled with that stuff for years myself, and that's why I do what I do now."*

Her eyes immediately filled with tears, and at that moment I thought to myself, *"What the hell did you just do, Carl?"* Dang upper brain—thanks a lot.

Recognizing the moment and knowing I had to get this situation back on the rails, I said, *"Hey, I know that's hard to hear, but do you want a daddy who lies to you or one who's going to be honest with you, no matter what?"*

She looked at me with tears in her eyes and replied, *"I want an honest daddy."*

I smiled and said to her, *"Well, that's what you got."*

She looked up and smiled and asked me, *"Is it OK if this upsets me a little bit?"*

I smiled and reassuringly responded, *"Of course. I understand. But I'm glad I can be honest with you."*

Despite that being one of the most difficult conversations of my adult life, it also proved to be a moment that brought my daughter and me even closer together. That display of honesty showed her that she could really trust me as her father. And as uncomfortable and awkward that conversation proved to be, it was one of the most valuable ones I've ever had.

Yeah, shame got really REAL for me that night. There was no denying it. And the only way I was able to get past it was by recognizing that familiar feeling and "acting as if" it had no hold on me.

There will always be moments in your life when the feelings of shame will well up inside you. You simply can't avoid it. But when it happens, you will be faced with a choice.

Do you obey your shameful inclinations and hide?

Or...

Do you do what's needed for the purposes of greater growth? Do you act "as if" that shame never existed in the first place?

Act As If

Like it or not, by now one thing should be clear: shameful feelings are inevitable. Yes, the degree of shame can vary from person to person, but we all experience it in one form or another in certain situations because we have all faced moments of rejection, loss, abandonment, and even abuse. In a word, we all have dealt with degrees of trauma. And so when we are triggered by a certain person, conversation, or surroundings, feelings of shame will arise because it's a completely natural emotional response.

Great. I thought this book was supposed to help me get rid of shame, not just reinforce the inevitably of it. Can I get a refund?

Maybe that's the thought you are having right now. And if so, I have two things for you:

First, read the cover again. This book is supposed to help you "conquer" your shame, not eliminate those feelings altogether. So sorry—no refund. :(

Second, just because we all experience shame, it does not mean we have to let it take over.

There's a huge difference between experiencing feelings of shame and allowing yourself to live in that shame. To put it another way, we can act on what we know rather than on what we feel.

When my daughter asked me about my past porn use, I felt ashamed. There's no getting around it. No one is immune to shame, and I certainly wasn't in that moment of mini-crisis. But I also knew what I was feeling was a betrayal of my best interests (and my daughter's). I knew that my mind's manager was running around the office half naked, freaking out, and pouring kerosene on everything with a lit match in hand, and what was really needed was for my CEO to come in and set things straight.

How did I know this? How could I be confident that what I was feeling was a lie that needed to be rejected?

It came down to two things: I knew the truth, and I knew what I truly valued.

And I'll tell you this. When you have your values right and you know the truth (and believe the truth), you can accomplish a lot that may seem impossible, or at least extremely difficult, when faced with your own crisis events.

You can **Act As IF**.

Yes, the fear of my daughter's anticipated rejection was significant, and it was a real possibility. I had no idea how she would take the news that her beloved father was once a "porn-addicted pervert." Or at least that's the narrative I pondered as I visualized all the potential catastrophic outcomes that would spill out from my honesty. But...

I knew the truth.

The truth was my sins and past mistakes were truly in the past.

The truth was I was forgiven and I had both purpose and value.

The truth was that my brokenness was no greater or lesser than someone else's.

The truth was God loved me, and that even if my daughter rejected me, I was not a reject.

But still, could I do it? Knowledge is power, but power still needs to be wielded for it to be of any effect. The hard reality was it didn't matter if I thought I could do it. I had to do it because...

I knew what I valued.

I valued my integrity and transparency.

I valued my daughter enough not to lie to her.

I valued my calling and journey.

I valued her opinion, but only if it wasn't based on a lie.

And so, armed with truth and my values, I did what was needed. I "acted as if," and I have never regretted that choice since. Understand when we choose to "act as if," there are two huge benefits to doing so.

First, there's the most obvious one. You conquer the challenge that you face in the moment. For me, the win was being honest with my daughter and the resulting bond that honesty formed. Likewise, when I shared with my son my own embarrassing experience involving masturbation, my win was improving the rapport I had with my son while also making sure he was educated on the topic by someone other than some punk at his school.

But then there's a second, more important benefit. You take a huge bite out of the shame that is trying to hold you back, weakening its power. In other words, the longer you act as if you feel no shame, the less shame you will eventually feel without needing to act at all. In layman's terms, *fake it 'til you make it*.

Admittedly, "faking it 'til you make it" sounds like an odd suggestion when I've been pressing so much for the need of transparency and honesty. Seriously, how could "faking it" ever be a good idea? But in this case "faking it" isn't meant to imply dishonesty, trickery, or deception. Rather, what I am talking about is a technique that was suggested by psychotherapist Alfred Adler, the father of Adlerian Theory, to aid clinicians in helping their patients take on new roles for development.

Adler asserted that when someone has difficulty acting pro-socially, that is, speaking assertively or responding with some measure of empathy, the clinician might encourage his patient to act "as if" he were assertive or empathic several times a day until the next visit. The logical basis for this reconstruction strategy is that as someone begins to act differently and to feel differently, he becomes a different person.[21]

Simply put, if you choose to act as if you are a different person, you can become a different person. Meaning, if you choose to act as someone who doesn't let shame control your life, eventually you will actually become a person who doesn't let shame control your life. I can tell you that, in my case, this is exactly how it's worked for me.

Realize that I never told anyone about my porn addiction until I was thirty-eight years old. The shame of admitting my addiction to anyone was just too great. But as I've grown in my freedom and shared with more and more people about my journey, talking about past porn use or masturbation issues has become almost as easy as talking about what I had for breakfast this morning. (I had oatmeal, by the way.)

I don't possess any special super power. There's nothing unique or extraordinary about me. I have the same lower and upper brain as anyone else, and am just as subject to the feelings of shame as you or the person standing next to you. But I refuse to let shame have the last word in my life, and so I behave accordingly. In essence, rather than being content to just wish I could live with less shame, I chose to become a person who lives with less shame.

Chapter 11

DEEP WORK

If you have no real faith background, this may not land with you, but if you've grown up in the church or attended a church for some time, then I think you might relate to this story. Like I said earlier, anxiety was a huge struggle for me. And to be honest, I still deal with it from time to time but not as badly as before. Regardless, when my anxiety was the worst, I wanted nothing more than someone to walk me through the process of conquering it so I could go back to simply enjoying my life.

One Sunday morning, I went to church as I normally did, but that morning the pastor got up and announced that his sermon would be on the topic of anxiety. Eureka! I had just hit the jackpot, or so I thought. His message was roughly thirty minutes long, and the bulk of it boiled down to the need to give our worries over to God. It was pretty typical of what I've heard in the past, and it left me feeling fairly flat.

I was so stoked at the beginning of the service, thinking I was finally going to get the key to unlocking my anxiety, but after the service concluded and the pastor said, "Amen," I walked away thinking to myself, *"Well, that was a waste of time."* I imagine what I felt in that moment was similar to the experiences of someone who got suckered into buying the latest As Seen on TV product.

Mind you, there was nothing wrong with what my pastor said. And the message wasn't lame or filled with fluff or anything like that. The problem was it completely missed my issue. See, while I knew that I struggled with hardcore anxiety, I had no idea why. The only reason I knew I was anxious was because of the physical symptoms I was experiencing such as chest tightness, lightheadedness, acid reflux, dizziness, and shortness of breath. But if you had asked me what I was so anxious about, my answer would have been, *"I have no freaking clue."* And so advice on how to release my cares to God was hollow at best—I wasn't consciously aware of the "cares" I apparently had been carrying around with me to begin with.

It wasn't until I broke down and started going to counseling that I saw improvement. It wasn't fast or overnight, but through the long process of weekly counseling, I was able to slowly crack open my mind and heart and figure out what I was suppressing all those years. It wasn't fun and it wasn't easy, but it was needed.

The bottom line is this: I wasn't able to experience a breakthrough until I committed to the **deep work** needed for that breakthrough. And if you struggle or have struggled with shame in the past, the key to moving past it and finally "acting as if" is going to be found only if you engage in some deep work yourself.

It's one thing to know that...

- Hiding from your shame and flaws is damaging.

- You need community and safe relationships to find healing.

- Your values and truth will help you get through the challenges you face.

- The damaging power of language lies in the shameful stuff we attach to it.

- We are all able to "act as if" and hold shameful thoughts at bay.

It's quite another to be able to identify the sources of shame in your life, define your values and truth, and gain the awareness needed to distinguish toxic shameful feelings from the truth of your reality.

Ultimately, to conquer the shameful feelings surrounding sex, porn, and masturbation, you need to do the deep work of diagnosing the shame and identifying those lies in the first place. And while no one can do that deep work for you, there is a process you can follow to help ensure you get to the desired destination.

Who Are You?

Before you get too far down the road of identifying and dealing with the shame in your life, you need to start with a basic question that faces all of us: Who are you?

Or to put it another way, where does your sense of identity come from?

This is a vital matter when it comes to addressing shame in your life, because until you recognize what you find your identity in, you can't establish your truth and values. You can't draw boundaries and build trust. You can't form meaningful goals.

Identity is key to the whole thing.

"Duh, Carl! Haven't you read your Bible? My identity is in Jesus, of course."

Yeah, yeah ... noted.

Regardless of your faith background or lack thereof, understand that what we say and what we truly believe can vary greatly. And it's important we recognize that what we truly believe will be evidenced by our behavior and not by what verse we can recite.

Because let's be real—what does "finding our identity in Christ" mean, anyway?

Christians say it all the time.
Pastors preach it constantly.
We read it in the Bible.

But have you ever stopped and thought really hard about what that actually means?

Well, before we answer that question, we need to go back to where it all began, the Garden of Eden. Recognize that the creation story is far more than a historical record of the earth's formation. In fact, some might argue it's not a historical record at all. But whether you believe God created the earth in seven literal days or not, the real significance of humanity's beginnings can be found in a little phrase found in the last verse of Genesis chapter 1: *"God saw all that he had made, and it was very good."*

The reason this is so significant is that God declared his creation to be good, not based on what it had done, what it had or hadn't accomplished, or whether people agreed with that evaluation. Nope. Apparently what made us and everything about this world good was the fact that God made it. In other words, his evaluation of us was not tied to any key performance indicators of any sort.

It was just good.

Now of course we all know what happened after that. Man decided that he knew better than God and ended up screwing up the whole thing. Needless to say, what once was good simply because God had deemed it so was now horribly marred and twisted. And rather than trusting God's good story and resting in his provision, man was now focused on getting ahead by any means necessary with little regard for the damage inflicted on others along the way.

This is why we need Jesus.

Because only he can do what we will always fail to do. Only he can fully accomplish the will of his father, while the absolute best we can hope for is to come up a little less short than the last time, but still short nonetheless. Only he can usher in God's new kingdom while inviting us to be an imperfect part of the process.

And so when Paul says in Ephesians, *"You were taught, with regard to your former way of life, to put off your old self, which is being corrupted by its deceitful desires;* **to be made new** *in the attitude of your minds; and to* **put on the new self***, created to be like God in true righteousness and holiness,"* the assumption and understanding is that **we are going to continue to come up short** in our efforts to walk out our new identity in Christ, but because of Jesus, we will be fully redeemed and again declared "good."

So when we base our identity on what we do or don't do, on what we say or don't say, on what we accomplish or fail to accomplish, on our performance or lack of performance, we invalidate any expressed belief that our identity is in Jesus and Jesus alone.

We must come to grips with our true identity before we can move on to anything else. Because when we choose to believe that our actions and/or relationships are what give us our identity, we cheapen that identity. We take something that has a set declared value and make it subject to the whims and views of those around us. And rather than having a static and secure definition to build our values and truth around, our identity and self-worth become as fickle as weather patterns, giving shame the foothold it needs in our minds and hearts.

I believe this applies whether you believe in Jesus or not. Your identity can't be based on your performance. It must be based on something that is fixed and certain.

What you struggle with does not define you.

What people expect of you does not define you.

What you achieve or fail at does not define you.

Your shame does not define you.

In the end, what does define you and your identity is a Creator who loves you unconditionally and has already deemed you as "good." How you choose to walk in that identity is entirely up to you.

Start with Your Why

In 2009, author and thought leader Simon Sinek released his book *Start with Why: How Great Leaders Inspire Everyone to Take Action*. This best-selling leadership book has sold over 170,000 copies, and his TED Talk based on the book has been viewed by over 28 million people, making it the third most popular TED video of all time.

Sinek's *Start with Why* makes the claim that the leaders and businesses who've had the greatest influence in the world, seen the greatest success, and generated the most loyal following operate with a very simple guiding principle:

> *People won't truly buy into a product, service, movement, or idea until they understand the WHY behind it. What you do is simply proof of what you believe.*

And while this concept is particularly important if you run a company looking to dominate the marketplace like Apple, or you're leading a movement determined to change the landscape of modern society, it's just as important for you and me as individuals, because all of us have a WHY.

Our WHY is what inspires us. It's what we are most passionate about at our core and sets us apart from everyone else. Most importantly, it's what motivates us to take action, and it guides our decisions.

Unfortunately, many people don't know what their WHY is because they don't have a clear understanding of their true identity and purpose. So they spend most of their lives going through the motions, doing whatever they need to do to get through each day's challenges. In the process, they lose sight of what really matters. Since they can't articulate their WHY, they are less likely to engage in the deep work needed for self improvement and real change since those efforts don't connect with anything of immediate significance in their lives.

But when someone does know their WHY, life gets a little simpler. Values start to crystallize and become clearer. What once was a hard choice now becomes the obvious and only choice, because a person's WHY serves as the lens through which all options are weighed and all decisions are validated.

Therefore, it is critical you take the time needed to discover your WHY and create what Sinek calls your WHY statement.

Think of your WHY statement as your life's mission statement. It should be simple, clear, actionable, focused on how you'll contribute to others, and expressed in a way that *resonates with your true identity.*

For example, my WHY statement is this:

To help people get the most from their lives and reach their greatest God-given potential, so that they in turn can help others do the same.

See, my WHY statement dictates everything else.

It's why I run a ministry focused on helping people find freedom from sexual brokenness.

It's why I have difficult talks with my kids and friends that encourage growth.

It's why I am willing to put myself out there when it comes to my past mistakes.

It's why I taught group training classes for three years in a gym.

It's why I've coached and mentored men over the past ten years.

And it's why I wrote this book.

Because what gets me out of bed each day isn't the smell of coffee (although that helps), but the ideal and hope that I can impact someone's life and help him move forward, even if it's just one small step.

Figure out your WHY.

Maybe it's inspiring people, like Simon Sinek.

Maybe it's providing for your family.

Maybe it's serving the needs of others.

Regardless of what it is, when you know it and own it, you'll be able to form meaningful goals, identify what you truly value, and articulate your individual truth with boldness and clarity, giving you a guiding influence when facing difficult conversations, uncomfortable choices, or feelings of shame that seek to hold you back.

Two Words

I don't know about you, but one thing I hate more than being ill or experiencing physical pain is not knowing why. I want to know the reason behind my ailment because then I have a place to start from when it comes to forming a recovery plan. But when a doctor comes in and says, *"We don't know; just let us know if it happens again,"* that drives me up a wall.

For instance, with most people, anxiety is tangible. They feel anxious and they know why. Maybe it's work, marriage, finances, the list goes on ... regardless, while they may not know how to remedy their anxiety, they at least have an idea as to what is driving those anxious feelings. For me it hasn't worked that way, and that is uber frustrating.

My point here is that we need a place to start if we are going to address the feelings of shame in our lives. Because even if we've begun to form a healthier understanding of our identity and can express our WHY, we still need to be able to recognize what drives our shame in the first place, and that means identifying its source. Another way to put it is that we have to figure out the origin of our shame to address our shame.

This isn't an easy process. It definitely takes work and will be painful at times. It very likely may require some professional guidance and help such as a therapist or counselor. But doing the deep work required to uproot shame's hold on you is worth every tear shed and drop of blood that may be spilled in the process.

And while I can't walk you through the actual work, I can tell you where to start looking for answers. Two words: *Conditional Love.*

Understand that love is a basic human need.

Love and belonging are part of Maslow's hierarchy of needs, a motivational theory in psychology that separates human needs into five hierarchical tiers often depicted as a pyramid. These needs, as Maslow postulates, must be fulfilled for a human being to grow and realize or fulfill his talents and potentialities (self-actualization). And while love is not essential to survival as are breathing, water, or food, a person still needs to feel love and belonging in order to grow.

Love given without conditions is the purest form of love and makes us feel the safest. This is the type of love God has for us, a love that exists regardless of how we behave or act. However, in the real world, this type of love is in short supply. Rather, much of the love we seek and receive is given and/or withheld based on what we can do for someone else. In other words, there is a price to be paid.

Recognize that we all have relationships in our lives built on conditional love. Some are expected, such as those one has with an employer, where the value of an employee is dependent on his ability to perform and/or toe the company line. But then there are those relationships where the "What have you done for me lately?" mentality seems out of place and disrupts our expectations.

Sure, we all understand that a boss might care about someone only if he meets certain demands, but what about a parent, sibling, friend, spouse, or pastor? Aren't those people supposed to love us for who we are and not what we can do for them?

Sadly, this is often not the case.

Consequently, when we feel the pressure to perform or conform from those we feel closest to because failure to do so will result in the withholding of love and acceptance, it is especially painful and shame inducing. Sure, if I don't come through on a deadline, my boss will give me crap, because that's what bosses do.

But my parents, my friends, my spouse—why can't I seem to live up to their expectations? There must be something wrong with me. Parents should just love their kids, right? So if I have to do something more to receive that love, then it must be because there is something super flawed with me to begin with.

Conditional love is where the roots of shame originate.

Maybe it was a parent who expected too much out of you, and when you came up "short," you were told that you never were good enough anyway.

Maybe it was a childhood friend or kids at school who seemed to accept you only if you acted a certain way or said certain things because the authentic you was just a waste of space.

Maybe it's a spouse who wants to invest in the marriage only if you have something to offer him or her because it's crazy to expect your mate to simply love you for the person you are.

Maybe it's a leader or pastor who cares about you only when you can serve him in a specific capacity because if not, he really has better things to waste his time on than dealing with you and your needs.

And maybe it began with a parent or sibling's transactional acceptance, but later in life when you meet other people who display those same traits, you get triggered and reminded about your lack of worth, allowing the lies you've grown up with to be reinforced and strengthened.

Whatever the case, failure to earn love or the threat of losing out on love strikes at your core human need for safety and connection, so rather than placing the blame where it belongs, you take on the responsibility for maintaining those relationships and the blame when things inevitably go southward.

One quick caveat here: conditional love is not the same as a person who cares about you but asks you to live up to your responsibilities. For instance, if you go to strip clubs once a week and your wife says, "I just can't do this anymore; you need to stop this behavior or I'm going to leave," that's not conditional love—that's a lack of ownership on your part.

Therefore, it's critical you examine the relationships in your life. Do the love and acceptance you get from the people around you come with conditions or are they freely given? And if there is price, what is the cost of failure, and what do you believe that failure says about you?

This is where you begin because the answers to those questions will lead you to the truth. And truth is what you need in the struggle against shame, because if you allow systems of conditional love to manipulate your life, those systems will ultimately define your truth and erode your personal boundaries.

Lines in the Sand

Here's the problem. There will likely be relationships in your life that aren't easy to recognize as being based on conditional love. After all, when the going is good, it can be really good. It's not until crap hits the fan that you are able to separate the love that's pure and the love that costs.

Plus, the reality is that the type of relationships we're talking about, as fickle as they may be, are still valuable to us. They typically are with people we've formed strong bonds with, so the prospects of just severing or abandoning those connections are too painful to consider. Yet, we can't just continue down the same path of transaction-based relationships or we'll never be free of the systems that seek to define our worth and identity.

The solution? Tell the truth.

Steven Luff, a therapist and friend of mine (and probably one of the smartest guys I know), said it this way when it came to the question of separating the good from the bad when it comes to relationships:

Truth is the great corrector.

There's a reason we call it "the hard truth": because at times the truth is not only difficult to express, but it can also be just as difficult, if not more so, to hear. The truth has a way of setting all things straight and clearing the floor—it doesn't give way to compromise or allow for manipulation.

People who love you conditionally don't care about the truth; they care only about their version of the truth. It's their world and you're just living in it. And as long as you abide by their rules and live within the confines of their truth, life is good and the status quo lives to fight another day. But when you change the rules of engagement and approach them with honesty rather than acquiescing to their expectations, you'll quickly separate the sheep from the wolves.

When you speak your truth to someone else, it's basically like drawing a line in the sand. In essence, you are communicating what passes and what doesn't when it comes to the dynamics of your relationship. The truth establishes boundaries and clarifies expectations, so when you speak it to those who love you conditionally, you force them to make a decision without ever having to issue an ultimatum. Love me as I am, or don't "love" me at all.

Now I want to offer a word of caution when it comes to the truth.

This is not license to be a jerk. It's not your free pass to say whatever you like without regard for someone else's feelings. The truth must always be communicated in love and with grace. Some relationships can be redeemed when you speak your truth and confront the elephant in the room, and some can't.

You can be honest about who you are, what you want or expect, and what you are or aren't willing to do and be loving at the same time. Whenever Jesus confronted people, he did so with unconditional love, setting an example for us to model as well. The goal in these conversations is to strengthen bridges, not burn them. And if the other person opts to pour kerosene on the whole thing, be the one holding the fire extinguisher and not the match.

Either way, know that their conditional love is not about a shortcoming or lack of worth on your part; rather, it is about their pain, their past, and their toxic love patterns, because loving someone unconditionally is not the norm for many people. It's upside down and radical. It's what Jesus offers us and what we should always be striving for. And when you don't get it, don't be shocked, but at the same time, don't settle for less.

It Takes a Community

There's no denying it. The work of "deep work" is difficult. It's challenging. And it's a learning process that, in many ways, is never ending. But it's essential if you want to experience a degree of breakthrough and finally find yourself in a place where shame no longer has a position of power in your life.

But it's not something you want to take on alone.

Here's the problem. So many times in life when you want to make a change, you opt to make that journey solo. Why invite someone else into a process that may look a little clunky along the way? Why have someone present who can challenge you when you form opinions and conclusions that might be incomplete or misguided? And beyond that, why open yourself up to scrutiny should you falter in your efforts?

Yet that is exactly what you need to do to help ensure your success.

Again, we are not talking about an easy process. Redefining your identity, purpose, truth, and relationships can seem overwhelming at times. And it can leave you feeling very unsafe and uncertain. So having a supportive network of relationships to lean into when facing times of uncertainty is imperative.

Think about it.

You've lived most of your life one way or another. And whether that has been a healthy exercise or not, it's familiar. It's comfortable, and doing deep work is decidedly uncomfortable. Consequently, it's only natural to have questions and doubts about the process, and if you have no one to turn to in those moments, you may be more inclined to abandon the process. But when you have a supportive community of trusted friends who understand and want the best for you, they can help assure you of your direction and decisions.

Likewise, even if you have great resolve and are certain about the need for change, there will be obstacles to that change. There will be good days and there will definitely be bad days, days when what you cognitively understand does not connect or resonate with what you feel. The result? Discouragement and possible dissolution. Again, this is when your community can be of great assistance championing your purposes and affirming your progress.

Gradual change is just that: *gradual.* So when looking in the mirror, small improvements may not stand out to you. But do you know who will notice? The people in your community, because they are more objective and can see the bigger picture. They can serve as a lifeline when you feel the storms of life threatening to sink your ship.

Most importantly, a community can provide the one thing you need most when confusion and self-doubt threaten to overtake your progress: *safety.*

Because while you may tend to downplay your need for connection, it's an essential need for human beings. Communities, tribes, groups—they are a large part of what keeps you grounded and feeling safe.

UCLA professor Matthew Lieberman put it this way in his book, *Social: Why Our Brains Are Wired to Connect*:

> *Being socially connected is our brain's lifelong passion. It's been baked into our operating system for tens of millions of years.*[22]

So when you feel alone, confused, and unsure, you also feel unsafe. And when you feel continually unsafe, you tend to rely on your brain's primitive fight-or-flight instincts to navigate life's challenges rather than critically evaluating each situation on its own merits. You may skip the "deep work" and opt for the easy lay up.

This is why community is essential to recovery and finding freedom from shame.

Because it is the very lack of connection, the absence of love and acceptance, and the lack of community that create shame and may drive you to compulsive behaviors such as porn, masturbation, strip clubs, and more in the first place.

Chapter 12

THE ROAD AHEAD

I may be a lot of things (Lord knows I've been called a lot of things), but one thing I'm not is a mind reader—just ask my wife. Not normally. Yet in this case, I'm going to take an educated guess as to what might be running through your mind at this point in our journey together.

Maybe you're thinking something along the lines of this:

> *I get it. Shame isn't good. I need to do some work here. And a lot of the reason I've felt shame in the past is because of the people I met and experiences I've faced in my life. But you don't get it.*
>
> *You don't know my situation.*
> *You haven't walked in my shoes.*
>
> *If you only knew the mistakes I've made and the damage I've caused due to my poor choices, you'd see. My shame is not only reasonable, it's deserved. There is no coming back from this.*

Sounds about right? See, I've been there. I've thought those same thoughts and had those same doubts. And here's what I'll tell you:

Bullshit.

I know … language!? But seriously, in my opinion, that is the most appropriate and accurate word for this situation. Because the truth is, there is no good reason to feel shame, and there is no such thing as "gone too far" when it comes to God. And you need to understand and accept that fact if you want to *move forward* without shame being the blockade that prevents you from enjoying the life you were created to live.

Whether you are a person of faith or not, you were born with a blank slate and have the ability to alter your life's direction for better or worse. Just because you've headed down the wrong path, it doesn't mean you can't course correct and head down a new path. Yet so many people feel this is the case, including Christians, who in theory should know otherwise.

This is because they've grown up in unhealthy religious systems with flawed theologies, and they developed beliefs about God that are inaccurate and downright harmful. Those beliefs increase their shame and hopelessness. They are beliefs I've held myself.

Yes, God is just. He hates sin and will someday make all things right. And yes, he promises judgment and punishment for the "wicked." Yet he's also love. He's merciful and full of grace. And because of that, he made a way through Jesus to redeem our broken state, something he knows we can never do for ourselves.

The road ahead is filled with challenges and struggles. Traveling it demands effort, commitment, and some real grit. Most importantly, it requires sincere belief, a belief that you are not defined by your failures and your past choices, good or bad. They are part of your unique story, and that story can be redeemed for greater purpose and impact than you ever imagined.

Good News, Bad News

Do you want the good news or the bad news first?

That's a question I never enjoy getting because whatever the good news is, I know there is something coming that's going to detract from my enjoyment of the other. Personally, I always want the bad news first so I can get it out of the way, but I'm not giving you that option.

Here's the bad news.

There are consequences to our poor choices that are unavoidable, because there is always a price to be paid for the pain we inflict on others. So yeah, cheating on your wife may result in a divorce. Looking at porn and masturbating in your cubicle may result in the loss of your job. And lying about inappropriate conversations with the receptionist at the office may mean a loss of trust with your wife.

These unfortunate results of our actions are not a byproduct of God's desire to teach us a lesson or harm us. They are just the natural and inevitable outcomes of relational pain. Understand that while God loves you and forgives you, no matter what, there is always a price to be paid by you or by someone else for your poor behavior, because pain begets more pain.

I tell you this because the fallout of our bad decisions can serve as a source of great shame. What I mean is this: we often tend to view our negative consequences as validation of our flaws.

So your wife didn't just leave you because you were unfaithful; she left you because you are a terrible human being who proved that fact with your unfaithfulness.

You didn't get fired from your job because you were searching for porn at work; you got fired because you're a hopeless pervert and you finally got caught.

Your wife doesn't trust you just because you lied about some inappropriate behavior with a coworker; she doesn't trust you because you are a lying son of a bitch and she finally realized that.

See the difference?

When we are already filled with shame, the natural reaction is to view our dire circumstances created by our poor choices as proof of our degenerate character. This is nothing new; it's a common phenomenon and a type of thinking that existed in Jesus' day, too.

In John 9:1–7, we read a story about Jesus' interaction with a blind man where his disciples assumed that the man's blindness was indicative of something wrong with him, some sort of sin that he had committed or his parents had committed. In other words, he wasn't just unlucky; he was severely flawed, and his blindness evidenced that assumed fact.

But we read that Jesus shot their notion down, responding, *"It was not that this man sinned, or his parents, but that the works of God might be displayed in him."* After correcting his disciples, Jesus then went on to heal the man.

Why is this so significant? Because that's the **good news.**

Regardless of what we've done or haven't done, or who we've hurt or betrayed, and despite the poor circumstances we may find ourselves currently facing, Jesus stands ready to forgive us and restore us.

Notice that Jesus didn't go back in time and change the man's blind condition. The pain and hurt he faced due to living in a broken world with an imperfect body were still there. But now he had the opportunity to move forward with a new sense of hope and joy.

This is the heart of God. This is unconditional love in action offered to anyone with no strings attached or hurdles to overcome. Not only are we to bring our bad decisions and wrongdoings to him for forgiveness, we also need to bring the shame and guilt of those choices to him as well.

Not so that we can avoid the inevitable consequences of our behavior.

Not so we can escape the need to make amends and ask forgiveness from those we hurt or wronged.

Not so we can keep doing whatever we want because we have a "get out jail free" card in hand.

No, we bring our pains, mistakes, and the shame that is attached to them to God so he can heal us and allow us to move forward with a new story that serves as a testament to the incredible love he has for us.

Understand...

We all mess up and hurt people.

We all have to deal with the results of the pain we inflict.

But our consequences don't define us, and they don't have to determine how we move forward. Because God provided a path to complete restoration through Jesus; we just need to be humble enough to walk it.

Prideful Degradation

You'd think when dealing with people who struggle with a great deal of shame because of the mistakes they've made, "prideful" would not be a word used to describe them. After all, if all you do is degrade and debase yourself, how could pride ever come into the conversation? Especially when you consider the definition of "pride" that Merriam-Webster offers:

> **Pride:** a feeling that you *respect yourself* and deserve to be respected by other people; a feeling that *you are more important or better* than other people.

The truth is when we feel extreme shame, it's the exact opposite. We don't respect ourselves. We don't feel important, and we definitely don't see ourselves as being better than anyone. Yet, pride is the real issue that stops us from accepting and embracing God's love and forgiveness.

Because when we say, "God can't forgive or fix me," what we really are saying is "I can't forgive or fix me." Our unwillingness to crucify our shame on the same cross Jesus did is a reflection of a deep-seated belief that our opinion of ourselves is more important than the opinion of our Creator.

God, you say that I'm "good," but I know better.
God, you say I have value and purpose, but I beg to differ.
God, you say I'm forgiven, but sorry—your standards aren't quite as high as mine.

It's the ultimate irony.

We have a low view of ourselves, yet we refuse to look up. We want to be free of the shame because of the sins we've committed, but we deny the forgiveness that's readily available.

What we fail to realize is that the notion of self-forgiveness is a fallacy anyway. The forgiveness you can extend yourself, while it may help you feel a little better, is inconsequential and carries no real weight. There is no freedom in it. There is freedom only in the perfect forgiveness God offers, because he is the just judge who ultimately will set all things right when he restores his good world.

It's counterintuitive but extremely freeing when you understand this concept. We all naturally want to be able to wrap our heads around things. It's not comfortable to just accept and trust. How can I accept God's love and forgiveness when I have a hard time loving and forgiving myself? It makes no sense, until you understand the bigger picture of the Gospel and how God works—then it makes perfect sense.

I ran into a similar situation myself when it came to my fitness and eating regiment. Understand, I've worked out, off and on, for most of my adult life (more on than off, thankfully). I've done and created thousands of different workouts, been certified as a personal trainer, led group classes, and read multiple books on nutrition and exercise. And while I'm not an "expert," I would say I'm very educated on the subject.

Recently I turned fifty, and over the past two or three years, while I've been able to stay within a good weight range and thought I understood how calorie consumption and burn worked, I haven't seen much progress. I've kind of plateaued, and in fact, I have lost a small degree of muscle.

So, I decided to hire a trainer to help guide me through my nutrition and fitness journey, hoping he could figure out why I was stuck. Imagine my surprise when my trainer said the first thing he wanted me to do was to start eating more—a lot more! He also wanted to change up some of my workouts and to increase rest times. **All of this seemed completely opposite to what I had been doing.** I questioned him, but he swore that I just needed to trust his "say so." So I did.

About ten days into this process, I was getting concerned that nothing was happening and that I might actually be getting fatter. But rather than leaning on my own understanding of how things worked, I trusted my trainer and stayed the course. Imagine my surprise when I did my first weigh-in just two weeks later, and was told I put on over one pound of muscle and reduced my body fat by a full percent. In fact, my numbers across the board were better than they had ever been in the past five years.

At that point, I looked at my trainer and said, *"I'm sold. Whatever you say, I'm doing. I trust you."*

I know my fitness story may not seem like a perfect fit for what you might be dealing with in your life, but it's the same concept. Too often we ignore the promises and affirmations of God because we believe that we know better. And with God, more often than not, his promises seem counterintuitive and will push up against our comfort zones and our understanding of how the world works.

But we just need to accept and trust.

I can't forgive myself, but you say I'm forgiven.
I accept that and trust you.

I don't see how you ever can redeem the mess I made with my life, but you say all things are possible.
I accept that and trust you.

I can never understand how this shame I feel isn't deserved, yet you say to let it go.
I accept that and trust you.

I don't think people will ever accept the real me, but you say it doesn't matter because you accept me.
I accept that and trust you.

There is no place for pride on the journey to freedom from shame. We need to get over ourselves at the end of the day and start believing the promises of God. Because often the road ahead doesn't require just humility, it requires trust as well.

A Tale of Two Judases

Among the hundred different "sins" that can derail our lives and destroy relationships, nothing is more personal and painful than an act of betrayal. Almost everyone knows what betrayal is like, and it's never fun. Whether it's from a friend, employee, business partner, leader, or spouse, the feeling of that cold knife in your back is unforgettable.

Betrayal sucks. No one likes a "Judas."

One of the unique aspects of betrayal, I believe, is that both parties understand the severity of the act and the pain it causes. I think this is why in relationships where betrayal exists, the path to reconciliation is especially difficult. The betrayed has to wrestle with the deep and lasting wounds of the act, but the betrayer has to be willing to own the gravity of his decision and to be humble and trusting enough to accept the forgiveness he seeks to receive.

We've all been there, and as painful as those moments are, no one knows the sting of betrayal quite like Jesus.

Jesus had the unbelievable privilege of being betrayed by two of his closest friends. Not only that, they both betrayed him around the same time and at the moment of his greatest need. One was his treasurer Judas Iscariot, and the other one was "Jersey Pete," who at one time swore he would die for Jesus if the moment ever called for it.

As a westerner, I naturally gravitate toward viewing Judas as the bigger scumball of the two. After all, he betrayed his rabbi for thirty pieces of silver (although there was very likely a bigger motivation behind his act than just money). Yet, we need to understand that betrayal was nothing new to Jesus or to any Jew of that day. Much like today, people betrayed each other for all sorts of reasons, usually connected to financial or political gain. And for Judas, it was the same thing. In today's world, we might say what Judas did was "nothing personal, just business."

However, if you read this account with an understanding of rabbinic discipleship, you'll realize that what Peter did was far more significant and egregious, because Peter was Jesus' talmid (what we would call a student but with a much deeper connection). For a talmid to publicly dissociate with one's rabbi was an unthinkable offense, and it was a degree of betrayal far greater and more personal than most modern Americans can even conceptualize.

In other words, you just never did what Peter did. It didn't happen.

Severity aside, both men committed a deep wrong. They both betrayed their teacher, friend, and rabbi. And they both later recognized the heinous nature of their act. Yet, we know the story ends very differently for each of them.

Judas tried to give the money back, and when that failed, he went out and hanged himself. Simply put, he gave up. Rather than facing the consequences of his choices and seeking restoration, he chose to believe that his sins defined him and there was no coming back from what he did.

Peter, however, opted to walk a different path.

We read in John that when Jesus finds Peter, he's fishing. This piece of information is significant because it shows that Peter recognized his days as a talmid were over, so he returned to what he knew best: fishing. He understood there were consequences for what he had chosen to do and accepted that fact. But then Jesus does the unthinkable. He offers forgiveness and charges Peter with the task of "feeding his sheep" and leading his church.

And here is where the real difference between Judas and Peter can be seen.

While Judas in essence betrayed Jesus again by denying the possibility of his forgiveness, Peter simply took his rabbi at his word. Peter was willing to trust Jesus to give him a new tomorrow and renewed purpose. He believed that when his rabbi said he was worth saving and still fit to "feed his sheep," that it was so.

You don't see Peter saying, *"Hey, man, thanks but I don't know—do you realize what I did?"* No, he just accepted and trusted the words of his teacher. And that's what you have to do if you are still carrying around the baggage of shame and regret.

You need to believe your rabbi.
You need to trust the words of your Creator.

You need to stop worrying about forgiving yourself and just accept the superior forgiveness that's already accessible to you, because when you do, great things can happen. Peter owned his mistakes. He accepted the consequences. But he left the door open for a comeback and never shied away from his choices. And even though we don't see it explicitly stated in the Bible, I believe he shared his story and denied the shame attached to it as a testament to God's amazing and restoring love.

And you can do the same.

The Prodigal Pastor

Several years ago, I received a call from a pastor who was looking for help with assisting a member of his church with his pornography struggle. The conversation went very well, and after we got through the typical small talk and introductions, he told me that he had a heart for this stuff because he too had issues with porn years earlier but was now "free."

Awesome! Right?

Then he dropped this nugget on me. He continued to tell me that he was looking for help from "someone like me" because I was better suited to address this problem with his member than he was. I told him that I wasn't sure if that was the case since he had been through the same struggle and experienced victory in his life. He then replied, *"Yes, but I'm not comfortable telling that to people. That's a detail I don't really want to share"*

Wait ... what?

I really don't remember much else about that call or how things turned out, but I'll never forget what he said. Because for me, the idea of being "free" and still not being comfortable talking about his past struggle was incompatible. How can one claim freedom if he is still being held back by the shame of his past? That's a major disconnect for me.

And beyond that, this man was in ministry. How many opportunities to serve and help people had he missed out on because he was unwilling to say the words, *"Me, too"*? How many men and women in his church had been left feeling alone and misunderstood, when in reality, their lead pastor knew very well the realities of their plight and could have walked them through the process of healing and recovery? How much good could have been accomplished if that one-time prodigal pastor had been willing to stand up and say, *"Yeah, I get it. I've been there. I made mistakes myself, but there is a path to restoration, and I can help you find it"*?

I've been in this line of work for almost a decade, and one thing I hear over and over again is that people are far more inspired by those who've walked the path before them and have real life experience versus those who just talk about something because they've read a few books on the topic.

Empathy is powerful, but when you've "been there" yourself, that empathy carries a level of authority with it that's undeniable. Rather than being a person who has the ability to understand and share someone's feelings, he *is* a person who understands and shares those feelings because he's had the same experiences and faced the same pain.

Don't get me wrong—I understand the challenge that this pastor and all pastors face. I realize that in today's church world, if he had embraced his story fully, he could have quite frankly lost his job. Being a leader and holding a position of influence carries with it great responsibility and requires a certain level of discretion. But unfortunately, when we have life experiences that can be used to help others find hope and healing, remaining silent about our own past struggles does no one any good and ultimately will not help us break though the final barrier of the shame that limits our potential and influence.

The Porn Couple

About five years ago, my wife and I were invited to be part of an event at a church in Ohio. The name for the event was "Resentment," and the focus was on diving into the different areas of our lives where resentment had built up from broken relationships and past hurts. The hope was that we could help guide people toward a better way of living, a life free of resentment and the vices that many use to numb the pain of their unresolved hostilities.

This event was not about porn per se, but the host wanted a couple on their panel who had been through the pain of porn addiction and betrayal, so Katie and I got the call. Yes, we had officially become the "porn couple" in their group of guest speakers. I'm sure that's the dream of every little boy and girl out there.

The event turned out to be pretty cool. Understand that when it comes to church events, I don't hold my breath or expect much because I've been to wayyy too many lame ones. But this one was different, probably because the discussions we were diving into were not safe or sterilized, but they were pretty sticky and frankly uncomfortable. It was raw and unfiltered, and that's kinda my jam.

After the main speaker wrapped up his message, the group of panelists took the stage (my wife and me included). After we had settled in on our uncomfortable stools, the main speaker went around asking us each questions about our stories and how resentment and anger played into our lives and decisions. Then came the big moment: Time for questions from the audience!

To be truthful, most of the questions were directed toward other panelists regarding their brushes with suicide, abuse, and the like. Then one guy got up and said, "I have a question for the porn addict guy." (OK, he didn't say it that way, but you get the idea.) He then went on and asked me, *"How do you have the bravery to get up there in front of all these people and talk about your struggles with porn?"*

The mic got handed to me, I chuckled a little bit, and then I answered, *"Well, I'm from New Jersey, so I have an unfair advantage in that we often don't give a crap what people think."*

The crowd laughed a little, and then I continued.

"Honestly, I don't think of myself as brave. There's nothing brave about admitting I was a porn addict. Nothing is on the line here. I'm not jumping on a bomb or anything. But what allows me to do this is that I refuse to be ashamed of my story. I know I'm forgiven, and while I wouldn't say those choices were planned by God, he's used my experience to help others, and that's pretty cool. The truth is that most people think that when they struggle with secret sins, they need to hide because they lack integrity. But I believe that when someone is willing to step out and admits he needs help, is willing to own his crap, that's real integrity and should be applauded, not looked down on."

After the event wrapped up, all of the panelists hung out a bit to talk to people if they had questions. The ironic thing was that while my wife and I received the fewest questions from the crowd when we were up on stage, we by far had the most people come up to talk with us afterwards. All of them had stories of addiction and betrayal and were looking for help and direction. It was a humbling experience, and one that greatly affirmed our decision to be involved.

This is the power of sharing your story.

Real Influence

I'll be honest, I'm not a huge social media guy. Quite honestly, I think social media is a waste of brain power 99 percent of the time. Admittedly, I have accounts on all the major platforms (for people my age) such as Facebook, Instagram, Twitter, and LinkedIn, but that's mostly for work reasons. Don't get me wrong—I understand that social media offers some value to people, but most of what I see come across my feeds is garbage. I think the aspect of social media I hate the most is all the hype and focus centered on today's "influencers."

Sure, there are some people on social media who have a really powerful message and the cred to back up their status, but in my opinion, most "influencing" is from a bunch of people with strong personal (and often uneducated) opinions, a nice camera and mic, and some savvy marketing skills, but not much else. It's kinda crazy how in today's culture, Christians included, there's a whole generation of people who want nothing more than to make a living being an "influencer."

Like that's a career? For real!?

Regardless, that's the quasi-celebrity culture we find ourselves living in. We all want to be influencers on some level. If you ever doubted that, just read some of the two-sentence bios people include on their social profiles. I mean, even some pastors get into the action. Here's a small sample of some of my faves:

Founder I Podcast | ★ Money & Thought Leader | Trauma Clinician | LMHCA Therapist | ACC Trauma Coach | Coaching | Scholar | Fierce Men's Advocate

Pastor | Visionary Leader | Real Estate | Entrepreneur | Coach | Helping people build wealth in the 5 Capitals!

Bible Teacher, Leader, Thought Provoker, Influencer

OK, I'll stop there before we both want to vomit. My point here is not to rip these men and women, but to demonstrate that in today's world, the overriding sentiment seems to be that if I want to influence people and really matter, I need to make sure everyone knows how great I am.

It's hollow. It's posturing. And quite honestly, it's crap.

You know what you don't see people including in their little bios?

- *Former porn addict and chronic masturbator.*

- *Three-time loser and failed business owner.*

- *Still trying to figure crap out.*

- *Can't manage money well and working my way out of bankruptcy.*

- *Had multiple affairs but now working on my marriage.*

But those little headlines would be far more authentic and impactful, because that's real life. That's what people need: hope for a better future from someone who's been there. I can't really identify with an "uber-successful entrepreneur, visionary minded thought leader, and keynote speaker," but you know who I can identify with? The person who's had modicum of success after making a slew of mistakes along the way because they grinded it out and did the work.

Yeah, give me that person. I'll listen to them.

Influence isn't about how many podcast listeners you have, or how many views your latest TikTok video got as you pontificated about nonsense in the front seat of your car, or how many YouTube subscribers you can brag about, or even how many readers you've accumulated for your Medium blog.

No, influence is the ability to deeply impact someone's life.

Real influence can't be determined by analytics or click meters; it can be determined only by the results you see—changed lives. When it comes to the areas of sex, porn, and masturbation, real positive influence has never been more of a need. And the ones who are best fit to offer that influence are the wounded who've fought the battles, faced down the shame, and spilled some blood along the way. Let me follow those people, because they get it and they've lived it.

Maybe that's you?

And before you close this book and say, *"Sounds good, but not me."* Let me just say this.

Twenty years ago, my life looked very different than it does now.

- I was a raging porn addict.

- I often masturbated at work.

- I lied to my wife constantly about my browser history.

- I wasn't the most amazing dad.

- I worked at a job I hated and felt that I had no purpose.

- I flirted with women who weren't my wife.

- I had no accountability and didn't want it.

And I had zero interest in changing any of those realities.

Today I have the privilege of running an online nonprofit ministry dedicated to helping men and women find healing and freedom from porn and sex addiction.

- Our websites get 13,000 visitors a month looking for help.

- Our small groups program and online communities have served over 10,000 people.

- Our workshops have walked thousands through the process of recovery and healing.

- And now I wrote a book.

That's real influence.

But I'm not special. I don't have any sexual integrity superpowers. I'm not a genius, nor do I have the secret recipe for success. I don't lead a mega-church, nor is my speaking calendar filled up. And no, I don't have a $1,000 video master-class program I want to sell you at the end that guarantees you'll conquer the shame in your life (or your money back).

Nor are the personal stories I have chosen to share with you meant to be the gold standard by which you should model your life or expectations. I've offered you a peek into my world simply to let you see what it looks like in real life to navigate the minefields of shame and regret. Learn from my successes, and more importantly, learn from my failures. Because at the end of the day, your road is yours, and no one can travel it for you.

After all ... I'm just a guy from Jersey.

But what I do have is a commitment to not letting shame have the last say in my life. I believe in the power of sharing my story and a passion for helping others do the same. And I know that despite my mistakes and poor decisions, despite my many selfish choices, those moments and the redemption I've experienced since are part of my unique story that can be used to help others find freedom and purpose in their lives.

And your story can do the same. You just need to walk through that door and leave shame back where it belongs, in the dark sewer it crawled out of.

Let's go!

ADDITIONAL RESOURCES

Below, I've listed some additional resources that our ministries offer and also some that I am a huge fan of. All of these communities, courses, and books will help you on your journey to a shame-proof life because they hold a high view of sex and sexuality and also a commitment to helping people connect with others in their search for freedom and healing.

Support Communities

Small Groups Online
Whether you struggle with pornography and sexual sin, or you are married to someone who does, community must be an essential part of your journey toward freedom. True change—true transformation, true healing—begins to happen when people commit to walking this path (called life) together.

Small Groups Online offers more than sixty Christian online support groups that meet multiple times a day, every single day of the week, and this is your invitation to join us as we pursue freedom alongside one another.

Use the code *SHAMEFREE* and get your first month for free.

Visit www.smallgroupsonline.com for more information.

The Live Free Community

The Live Free Community offers a simple and safe way to bring men together who share a common struggle with porn, lust, or other unwanted sexual behaviors. Experience authentic community, find real accountability, and get access to exclusive content offering practical teaching, including expert interviews, free video workshops, and more—all in one place.

If you've felt alone and without hope, the Live Free app might be the very thing you need to change the game and bring freedom to your life.

Visit www.livefreecommunity.org for more information.

Live Free Wives

Live Free Wives is a completely free community that offers a safe and secure way to bring women together who share a common history of pain and sexual betrayal. Experience authentic sharing, find real support, and get access to exclusive content offering practical teaching, including expert interviews, free video workshops, and more—all in one place.

If you've felt alone and without hope, the Live Free Wives Community might be the very thing you need to bring freedom and healing to your life.

Visit www.livefreewives.org for more information.

Video Workshops and Courses

X3pure

This workshop is for both single and married men. If you are struggling with pornography or other unwanted sexual behaviors, the X3pure workshop is perfect for you. Private, online, and effective, the X3pure program can help you end the downward spiral of shame and alienation.

X3pure offers fifteen videos and a workbook, and it includes one year of Live Free Community access. Begin your recovery right now.

Visit www.x3pure.com for more information.

Christian Sexuality

Christian Sexuality is a twelve-part, video-based, comprehensive discipleship experience that will help youth leaders, mentors, and parents engage their youth in one of the most important conversations of our age—sex and sexuality.

This series is a powerful catalyst for healthy and meaningful conversations about sex, sexuality, and gender. It will guide you in the most pressing questions facing our culture today.

Visit www.christian-sexuality.com for more information.

The Very Good Sex Talk

This ten-day course includes short videos intended to help you as a parent (or grandparent) to better engage in the conversations surrounding sex and sexuality. It will help you explore God's design for sex and prepare you for the dialogue that will be needed in the years ahead. Every video comes with a worksheet, helpful handouts, and other tools for continued dialogue.

Visit www.projectsix19.org/the-very-good-sex-talk for more information.

Books

Wife Magnet: Become the Husband She Can't Keep Her Hands Off

Every month, over 21,000 people google the phrase "sexless marriage" looking for answers. Looking for hope. Looking for anything. Hope is here. In this groundbreaking bestselling book, you'll learn the real reason women pull away emotionally and sexually before leaving for good and how to move your marriage from cold-and-distant to close-and-intimate!

Visit www.wifemagnet.me for more information.

Unwanted: How Sexual Brokenness Reveals Our Way to Healing

This is a ground-breaking resource that explores the "why" behind self-destructive sexual choices. The book is based on research from over 3,800 men and women seeking freedom from unwanted sexual behavior, whether it's the use of pornography, an affair, or buying sex.

Visit www.jay-stringer.com/book for more information.

ADDITIONAL RESOURCES 227

The Great Sex Rescue: The Lies You've Been Taught and How to Recover What God Intended
In this book, Sheila Gregorie explores modern-day evangelical church sexual culture and how it leads to lower orgasm rates, less marital satisfaction, and even higher rates of sexual pain while offering evidence-based, Christ-centered sex advice. This is a must-read for women and men.

Visit www.tolovehonorandvacuum.com/great-sex-rescue for more information.

Grace-Based Recovery: A Safe Place to Heal and Grow
This small-group study is designed to help people suffering from addiction and those close to them understand God's grace and why it is the only path to true freedom.

With nine easy-to-use lessons, *Grace-Based Recovery* highlights the significant differences between a performance-based approach to recovery and a grace-based approach, and it establishes a safe environment where addicts can learn from their mistakes rather than be punished for them.

Visit www.grace.bebroken.com for more information.

NOTES

[1] J. Terrizzi Jr. and N. Shook, 2020. "On the Origin of Shame: Does Shame Emerge From an Evolved Disease-Avoidance Architecture?" *Frontiers in Behavioral Neuroscience*, 14, pp. 1–2.

[2] Ibid.

[3] L. Dolezal and B. Lyons, 2017. "Health-Related Shame: An Affective Determinant of Health?" *Medical Humanities*, 43(4), pp.257–263.

[4] Ibid.

[5] Ibid.

[6] P. Stiles and R.S. Manager. Working Paper Series. "The Negative Side of Motivation: The Role of Shame."

[7] C. Feiring, 2005. "Emotional Development, Shame, and Adaptation to Child Maltreatment." *Child Maltreatment*, 10(4), p. 309.

[8] Harvard Business Review. 2021. "Don't Let Shame Become a Self-Destructive Spiral." Available at: https://hbr.org/2017/06/dont-let-shame-become-a-self-destructive-spiral [accessed 23 July 2021].

[9] C. Feiring, op cit., p. 308.

[10] Amsale Cherie and Yemane Berhane. "Oral and Anal Sex Practices among High School Youth in Addis Ababa, Ethiopia." *BMC Public Health* 12, no. 1 (2012). https://doi.org/10.1186/1471-2458-12-5.

[11] Ibid.

[12] Josh McDowell. *The Porn Phenomenon: The Impact of Pornography in the Digital Age.* Barna Group, 2016.

[13] Shaohai Jiang and Annabel Ngien. "The Effects of Instagram Use, Social Comparison, and Self-Esteem on Social Anxiety: A Survey Study in Singapore." *Social Media + Society*, vol. 6, no. 2, 2020, p. 205630512091248., doi:10.1177/2056305120912488.

[14] "The Asch Experiment: The Power of Peer Pressure" (February 20, 2021). Retrieved September 7, 2021, from https://socialsci.libretexts.org/@go/page/8114

[15] Shaohai Jiang and Annabel Ngien. Op cit.

[16] Ibid.

[17] Rbs. "2020 Year End Report Data Breach QuickView." Risk Based Security, 2021, www.riskbasedsecurity.com/quickviewreports/.

[18] JS Bowers and CW Pleydell-Pearce (2011). "Swearing, Euphemisms, and Linguistic Relativity." PLOS ONE 6(7): e22341. https://doi.org/10.1371/journal.pone.0022341

[19] Caroline Hachem. "Let's (Not) Talk About Sex: An Exploration of Taboo and Politeness in Modern Peninsular Spanish" (2017). LSU Master's Theses. 4390. https://digitalcommons.lsu.edu/gradschool_theses/4390

[20] Herbert Alexander Simon. *Reason in Human Affairs*. Stanford University Press, 1990.

[21] Richard E. Watts, et al. "Expanding the Acting As If Technique: An Adierian/Constructive Integration." http://www.centroadleriano.org, The University of Texas Press, 2005, http://www.centroadleriano.org/wp-content/uploads/2016/04/Expanding.pdf.

[22] Matthew Lieberman. *Social: Why Our Brains Are Wired to Connect*. Crown Publishers, 2013.

www.ingramcontent.com/pod-product-compliance
Lightning Source LLC
Chambersburg PA
CBHW032223080426
42735CB00008B/685